# Excel
## Get the Results You Want!

# Years 5-6
# Selective Schools
# and Scholarship Tests
# Skills and Strategies

Lyn Baker, Sharon Dalgleish,
Tanya Dalgleish, Donna Gibbs
& John Moir

PASCAL
PRESS

© 2023 Lyn Baker, Sharon Dalgleish, Tanya Dalgleish, Donna Gibbs, John Moir and Pascal Press

**Completely new edition incorporating late 2020 Selective School test changes**

Reprinted 2024

ISBN 978 1 74125 638 3

Pascal Press Pty Ltd
PO Box 250
Glebe NSW 2037
(02) 9198 1748
www.pascalpress.com.au

Publisher: Vivienne Joannou
Project editor: Mark Dixon
Edited by Mark Dixon and Rosemary Peers
Proofread by Mark Dixon
Answers checked by Dale Little and Peter Little
Cover by DiZign Pty Ltd
Typeset by Grizzly Graphics (Leanne Richters)
Printed by Vivar Printing/Green Giant Press

# Contents

## ABOUT THIS BOOK

This book has been written to help develop students' skills and strategies in tackling Selective Schools and Scholarship Tests. The aim of this book is to identify, develop and practise skills and strategies which will be useful in test situations, and, in particular, for the NSW Selective High School Placement Test and the ACER Scholarship Tests (Secondary Level 1).

This book will help students organise their thinking—creatively and systematically—when faced with tests, with the object of helping them become more effective and independent thinkers.

Note: There can be no guarantee of 'carry-over' of a particular skill or strategy from one situation or problem to another. However, there is little doubt that practice can at least make 'closer to perfect' and should certainly lead to a child gaining greater familiarity and confidence when taking a test. The strategies included in this book will go beyond that and provide the basis for the positive attitude so necessary to being successful.

The book is divided into two parts. Part 1 (Year 5) and Part 2 (Year 6) consist of the following:

**1 Explanation pages**

These include:

- the skill to be practised
- an explanation that relates the skill to the types of test questions
- practice questions
- suggested solutions and strategies.

**2 Sample questions**
These are follow-up questions to practise the skills covered in the explanation pages.

**3 Sample tests**
At the end of Year 5 and Year 6 there are sample tests for students to practise based on the NSW Selective High School Placement Test.

**4 Answer pages with explanations**
These include additional suggested methods to help with the student's thinking in answering the questions.

## BACKGROUND TO SELECTIVE TESTING

Tests for entry into selective government schools were introduced in order to provide an opportunity for pupils with scholastic aptitude. Over 15 000 applications are made for the just over 4000 selective places available and entry is quite competitive. It is not unusual for some primary schools not to be able to place even one of their pupils into a selective school.

The tests were updated in late 2021 with a greater emphasis on literacy, thinking skills, mathematical reasoning and problem solving. The General Ability Test has been replaced by a Thinking Skills Test. The new Selective High School Placement Test adjusts and balances the weighting given to the Reading, Thinking Skills, Mathematical Reasoning and Writing components. These changes were in response to the findings of the 2018 Review of Selective Education Access report, commissioned by the NSW Department of Education.

The tests are designed to assess higher-level reasoning. The main emphasis is on thinking with words, numbers and ideas. The reason for the emphasis on English and Mathematics is that they are considered to be predictors of high-school achievement.

## ABOUT THE SELECTIVE SCHOOL TEST

The NSW Selective High School Placement Test consists of four sections:

- **Reading** (30 questions in 40 minutes)
- **Thinking Skills** (40 questions in 40 minutes)
- **Mathematical Reasoning** (35 questions in 40 minutes)
- **Writing** (one question in 30 minutes).

The tests, except Writing, are in multiple-choice form, with each question being of equal value. Marks are awarded for each correct answer and applicants are advised to guess the answer if they are uncertain.

Although there are similarities in the content

of the NSW Selective High School Placement Test and the ACER Scholarship Tests, since the Selective Schools Test format changed in 2020 there are now more differences.

## HOW THE RESULTS ARE USED BY PUBLIC SCHOOLS

Entry to selective high school is based on academic merit. In 2022 changes were made to the allocation of places. Under the Equity Placement Model, up to 20% of places are held for members of the following disadvantaged and under-represented groups:

- students from low socio-educational advantage backgrounds
- First Nations students
- rural and remote students
- students with disability.

It is important to remember that the places allocated under the Equity Placement Model will not necessarily be filled. In 2023, the first year of this new system, less than 10% of these places were offered. This means that more than 90% of the places were offered to general applicants. The new system has helped close the educational gap in participation from disadvantaged groups without having a significant impact on other applicants.

Students no longer receive a test score or placement rank. The new performance report will instead place students in one of the following categories:

- top 10% of candidates
- next 15% of candidates
- next 25% of candidates
- lowest 50% of candidates.

This change addresses privacy and wellbeing concerns including unhealthy competition between students. The sole purpose of the test is to identify students who would benefit from the chance to study at a selective school and, since it doesn't test knowledge of the curriculum, there is no diagnostic merit in the test—unlike the NAPLAN test, which can help identify areas where children can improve.

Minimum entry scores for selective schools are no longer published because these change from year to year and depend on the number of applicants, their relative performance and the number of families who decline an offer. Students placed on the reserve list no longer receive a numerical rank; instead an indication of how long it will take to receive an offer, based on previous years, is provided.

A selection committee for each selective high school decides which students are to be offered places. These committees also decide how many students are to be placed on the reserve list. Should a student with a confirmed offer turn down a place at a selective school, the place will be offered to the first student on the reserve list.

There is an appeals panel for illness or other mitigating circumstances. All applicants are advised of the outcome. The NSW Government provides detailed information on the application and selection process for parents on the Selective High School Placement Test. This is available from: https://education.nsw.gov.au/parents-and-carers/learning/tests-and-exams/selective-school-test. Sample test papers are also available on this website.

## ABOUT THE SCHOLARSHIP TESTS

The ACER Scholarship Tests, which are usually held around May, are coordinated by the Australian Council for Educational Research (ACER). This testing is for entry to around 200 independent schools. About 15 000 students throughout Australia sit these tests. The tests cover three levels:

- Level 1: the last year of primary school (Year 6)
- Level 2: the second year of high school (Year 8)
- Level 3: Year 10 in high school.

Each private school awards its own scholarships. You can put your name down for more than one school but you will need a special registration form. There is also a separate fee for each school and you lodge your registration directly with the school and not with ACER.

You may be limited in the number of schools to which you can apply. This might happen if a school insists you have to sit for the test at their testing centre. Candidates usually sit the exam at the school which is their first choice. There are exceptions for country and interstate candidates.

The ACER Scholarship Tests comprise:

- Test 1: Written Expression (25 minutes)
- Test 2: Humanities—Comprehension and Interpretation (40 minutes)
- Test 3: Mathematics (40 minutes)
- Test 4: Written Expression (25 minutes).

## HOW THE RESULTS ARE USED BY PRIVATE SCHOOLS

The results are used by private schools to select students who have applied for a scholarship. Typically the highest scorers are considered first, together with any additional background information that might have been provided. It is important therefore to provide as much detail as possible in the application form to assist the selection committee in deciding between pupils who may have similar scores.

## ADVICE TO STUDENTS

Each question in the NSW Selectve Schools Placement Test is multiple choice except for the Writing Test. This means you have to choose the correct answer from either four or five options. You need to read the question in the test booklet then mark your answer on a separate answer sheet.

We have included sample answer sheets in this book—similar to those you will be given in the actual test—for you to practise on.

Under time pressure and test conditions it is possible to miss a question and leave a line on the answer sheet blank. Always check that your answer on the separate answer sheet is written down next to the right number. For instance, check that your answer to question 15 is written down against the number 15 on the answer sheet.

There is nothing worse than finding out you have missed a space, especially when time is running short.

## ADVICE TO PARENTS

- **Practice:** There is no doubt that practice in the various kinds of tests and their individual categories can be a great help. This is partly because the brain is kept ticking over at a high level but also so it is unlikely your child will be faced with a kind of problem in the test with which they are unfamiliar.

- **Ask:** Please encourage your child to ask (a parent or teacher is probably best in these cases) if explanations in the book are insufficient for a clear understanding of a question or answer, or the processes involved in going from one to the other are unclear.

- **Time to think:** Do not expect your child to attempt more than one test at a time if they are to get the most out of each one. Apart from having a negative effect, there is little to be gained by this; it would be more beneficial to reflect on the mistakes (if any!) in the exercises just completed and how best to remedy these.

- **Be positive:** Don't be too critical of your child's attempts, particularly before they become used to the kinds of tests. Positive reinforcement—with considered and constructive criticism—will always be of greater benefit than any negative reactions, especially if you want your child to attempt—or even look forward to—another test in the future. We must, rather, look for ways to help children develop confidence in themselves as well as an enthusiasm for intellectual pursuits and for testing their intellect.

# Reading answer sheet

Mark your answers here.

To answer each question, fill in the appropriate circle for your chosen answer.

Use a pencil. If you make a mistake or change your mind, erase and try again.

You can make extra copies of this answer sheet to mark your answers to the two Sample Reading Tests in this book.

| | | | |
|---|---|---|---|
| 1 A B C D ○○○○ | 6 A B C D ○○○○ | 11 A B C D E F ○○○○○○ | 16 A B C D ○○○○ |
| 2 A B C D ○○○○ | 7 A B C D ○○○○ | 12 A B C D E F ○○○○○○ | 17 A B C D ○○○○ |
| 3 A B C D ○○○○ | 8 A B C D ○○○○ | 13 A B C D E F ○○○○○○ | 18 A B C D ○○○○ |
| 4 A B C D ○○○○ | 9 A B C D ○○○○ | 14 A B C D E F ○○○○○○ | 19 A B C D ○○○○ |
| 5 A B C D ○○○○ | 10 A B C D E F ○○○○○○ | 15 A B C D ○○○○ | 20 A B C D ○○○○ |

# Thinking Skills answer sheet

Mark your answers here.

To answer each question, fill in the appropriate circle for your chosen answer.

Use a pencil. If you make a mistake or change your mind, rub it out and try again.

You can make extra copies of this answer sheet to mark your answers to all the Sample Thinking Skills Tests in this book.

| | A B C D E | | A B C D E | | A B C D E | | A B C D E | | A B C D E |
|---|---|---|---|---|---|---|---|---|---|
| 1 | ○○○○○ | 7 | ○○○○○ | 13 | ○○○○○ | 19 | ○○○○○ | 25 | ○○○○○ |
| 2 | A B C D E ○○○○○ | 8 | A B C D E ○○○○○ | 14 | A B C D E ○○○○○ | 20 | A B C D E ○○○○○ | 26 | A B C D E ○○○○○ |
| 3 | A B C D E ○○○○○ | 9 | A B C D E ○○○○○ | 15 | A B C D E ○○○○○ | 21 | A B C D E ○○○○○ | 27 | A B C D E ○○○○○ |
| 4 | A B C D E ○○○○○ | 10 | A B C D E ○○○○○ | 16 | A B C D E ○○○○○ | 22 | A B C D E ○○○○○ | 28 | A B C D E ○○○○○ |
| 5 | A B C D E ○○○○○ | 11 | A B C D E ○○○○○ | 17 | A B C D E ○○○○○ | 23 | A B C D E ○○○○○ | 29 | A B C D E ○○○○○ |
| 6 | A B C D E ○○○○○ | 12 | A B C D E ○○○○○ | 18 | A B C D E ○○○○○ | 24 | A B C D E ○○○○○ | 30 | A B C D E ○○○○○ |

# Mathematical Reasoning answer sheet

Mark your answers here.

To answer each question, fill in the appropriate circle for your chosen answer.

Use a pencil. If you make a mistake or change your mind, erase and try again.

You can make extra copies of this answer sheet to mark your answers to all the Sample Mathematical Reasoning Tests in this book.

| | | | |
|---|---|---|---|
| 1 A B C D E ○○○○○ | 6 A B C D E ○○○○○ | 11 A B C D E ○○○○○ | 16 A B C D E ○○○○○ |
| 2 A B C D E ○○○○○ | 7 A B C D E ○○○○○ | 12 A B C D E ○○○○○ | 17 A B C D E ○○○○○ |
| 3 A B C D E ○○○○○ | 8 A B C D E ○○○○○ | 13 A B C D E ○○○○○ | 18 A B C D E ○○○○○ |
| 4 A B C D E ○○○○○ | 9 A B C D E ○○○○○ | 14 A B C D E ○○○○○ | 19 A B C D E ○○○○○ |
| 5 A B C D E ○○○○○ | 10 A B C D E ○○○○○ | 15 A B C D E ○○○○○ | 20 A B C D E ○○○○○ |

# Making a judgement about a character and their relationship with others

**ACTIVITY:** You must look at what each character says and does, and work out how the situation they are in affects how they act towards each other.

*Read the text below then answer the question.*

Doctor Dolittle was very fond of animals and kept many kinds of pets. Besides the gold-fish in the pond at the bottom of his garden, he had rabbits in the pantry, white mice in his piano, a squirrel in the linen closet and a hedgehog in the cellar.

[…]

His sister used to grumble about all these animals and said they made the house untidy. And one day when an old lady with rheumatism came to see the Doctor, she sat on the hedgehog who was sleeping on the sofa and never came to see him any more, but drove every Saturday all the way to Oxenthorpe, another town ten miles off, to see a different doctor.

Then his sister, Sarah Dolittle, came to him and said,

'John, how can you expect sick people to come and see you when you keep all these animals in the house? It's a fine doctor would have his parlor full of hedgehogs and mice! That's the fourth personage these animals have driven away … We are getting poorer every day. If you go on like this, none of the best people will have you for a doctor.'

'But I like the animals better than the "best people",' said the Doctor.

'You are ridiculous,' said his sister, and walked out of the room.

From *The Story of Doctor Dolittle* by Hugh Lofting

## SAMPLE QUESTION

How fond is Dr Dolittle of his patients?

A  very fond          B  not at all fond          C  quite fond          D  extremely fond

## STRATEGY

You need to **make a judgement** based on evidence about what the character (in this case, Dr Dolittle) does and says in the text and how he interacts with or relates to others (his patients). Think about the particular situation the characters are in and how this might affect their behaviour.

Dr Dolittle seems to take very little notice of his patients. He fills his home and treatment room with animals so it is not in a state fit for his patients to visit. He even confesses that he likes his animals more even than his 'best' patients.

His sister is annoyed with him and points out he is driving his patients away with this attitude. He doesn't appear to take much notice of her opinion.

Now look at options **A–D** and decide which best answers the question.

**B is correct.** There is plenty of evidence that Dr Dolittle is not at all fond of his patients.

**The other options are incorrect.** There is no evidence that Dr Dolittle is very fond of his patients, quite fond of his patients or extremely fond of his patients.

# Identifying the meaning of a word in context

**ACTIVITY:** You need to work out the context that gives meaning to the word. The context is everything that influences, acts upon or is connected with the word in the text.

*Read the text below then answer the question.*

> Doctor Dolittle was very fond of animals and kept many kinds of pets. Besides the gold-fish in the pond at the bottom of his garden, he had rabbits in the pantry, white mice in his piano, a squirrel in the linen closet and a hedgehog in the cellar.
>
> [...]
>
> His sister used to grumble about all these animals and said they made the house untidy. And one day when an old lady with rheumatism came to see the Doctor, she sat on the hedgehog who was sleeping on the sofa and never came to see him any more, but drove every Saturday all the way to Oxenthorpe, another town ten miles off, to see a different doctor.
>
> Then his sister, Sarah Dolittle, came to him and said,
>
> 'John, how can you expect sick people to come and see you when you keep all these animals in the house? It's a fine doctor would have his parlor full of hedgehogs and mice! That's the fourth personage these animals have driven away … We are getting poorer every day. If you go on like this, none of the best people will have you for a doctor.'
>
> 'But I like the animals better than the "best people",' said the Doctor.
>
> 'You are ridiculous,' said his sister, and walked out of the room.
>
> From *The Story of Doctor Dolittle* by Hugh Lofting

## SAMPLE QUESTION

What does 'ridiculous' mean?

**A** amusing          **B** monstrous          **C** unreasonable          **D** scatterbrained

## STRATEGY

Words can change their meanings in different contexts so it is essential to think about the context: who says it, where the word occurs and how it fits into the whole text.

'Ridiculous' usually means very silly or foolish. The context for the word 'ridiculous' in this text is that it is said by Dr Dolittle's sister, who is worried her brother's behaviour is driving away his patients. The word expresses her feelings of annoyance about his behaviour and his response to her pointing out its consequences. That she immediately walks out of the room after calling her brother 'ridiculous' shows she is angry with him. You can work out she thinks he is not being sensible.

Now look at options **A–D** and decide which best answers the question.

**C is correct.** It is the foolishness and short-sightedness of her brother's behaviour that annoys his sister. From her perspective he is being unreasonable about the situation.

**A is incorrect.** The Doctor's sister is not at all amused by the Doctor's attitude.

**B is incorrect.** There is no evidence that the Doctor's sister thinks her brother's behaviour evil or wicked, which the word 'monstrous' implies.

**D is incorrect.** Someone who is scatterbrained lacks the ability to concentrate and Dr Dolittle is certainly able to concentrate on his animals.

# PRACTICE QUESTIONS

*Read the text below then answer the questions.*

Doctor Dolittle was very fond of animals and kept many kinds of pets. Besides the gold-fish in the pond at the bottom of his garden, he had rabbits in the pantry, white mice in his piano, a squirrel in the linen closet and a hedgehog in the cellar.

[…]

His sister used to grumble about all these animals and said they made the house untidy. And one day when an old lady with rheumatism came to see the Doctor, she sat on the hedgehog who was sleeping on the sofa and never came to see him any more, but drove every Saturday all the way to Oxenthorpe, another town ten miles off, to see a different doctor.

Then his sister, Sarah Dolittle, came to him and said,

'John, how can you expect sick people to come and see you when you keep all these animals in the house? It's a fine doctor would have his parlor full of hedgehogs and mice! That's the fourth personage these animals have driven away … We are getting poorer every day. If you go on like this, none of the best people will have you for a doctor.'

'But I like the animals better than the "best people",' said the Doctor.

'You are ridiculous,' said his sister, and walked out of the room.

From *The Story of Doctor Dolittle* by Hugh Lofting

1  How does Sarah feel about her brother's behaviour?
   A  admiring
   B  alarmed
   C  curious
   D  intrigued

2  What does the word 'personage' mean in the text?
   A  celebrity
   B  important person
   C  person who is very old
   D  visitor

☞ Answers and explanations on page 108

# Making a judgement about a character

**ACTIVITY:** You have to consider all the information you are given about the character: their words and actions, their relationships, and what others think or feel about them. You need to think critically about this information to make a judgement. Is what is said, for example, reliable, accurate, trustworthy or entertaining?

*Read this extract from a poem by Hilaire Belloc then answer the question.*

## Matilda

Matilda told such Dreadful Lies,
It made one Gasp and Stretch one's Eyes;
Her Aunt, who, from her Earliest Youth,
Had kept a Strict Regard for Truth,
Attempted to Believe Matilda:
The effort very nearly killed her,
And would have done so, had not She
Discovered this Infirmity.
For once, towards the Close of Day,
Matilda, growing tired of play,

And finding she was left alone,
Went tiptoe to the Telephone
And summoned the Immediate Aid
Of London's Noble Fire-Brigade.
Within an hour the Gallant Band
Were pouring in on every hand,
From Putney, Hackney Downs, and Bow
With Courage high and Hearts a-glow
They galloped, roaring through the Town
'Matilda's House is Burning Down!'

## SAMPLE QUESTION

Matilda is shown to be

A  a misunderstood young girl.

C  just like her aunt.

B  a disobedient, reckless child.

D  a victim of circumstance.

## STRATEGY

You need to weigh up how the poet presents the character (in this case, Matilda), how the character behaves and what others think of them to make a judgement.

The poem is full of drama with Matilda cast in the role of 'villain'. We learn she not only tells lies, but that her lies are quite shocking. Her Aunt confirms this and we have no reason to doubt her judgement. The amusing way her Aunt's despair is described (e.g. Attempted to Believe Matilda: / The effort very nearly killed her) emphasises Matilda's heartlessness. When Matilda is bored, she pretends the house is on fire and summons the Fire Brigade—a very wilful, thoughtless and potentially dangerous action. You judge that there is nothing at all to be said in Matilda's favour.

Now look at options **A–D** and decide which best answers the question.

**B is correct.** Matilda listens to no-one and does as she pleases without any care for the consequences. Her behaviour is both disobedient and reckless.

**A is incorrect.** There is no evidence that Matilda, although a young girl, is misunderstood. She tells lies and behaves recklessly.

**C is incorrect.** Matilda is not at all like her Aunt, who strongly disapproves of Matilda's lies and has a 'Strict Regard for Truth'.

**D is incorrect.** There is no evidence Matilda is a victim of any kind: she is the one controlling events and creating the circumstances.

# Predicting or forecasting what could occur based on evidence from the text

**ACTIVITY:** You need to guess what might happen next by using the evidence and hints you have been given so far.

*Read this extract from a poem by Hilaire Belloc then answer the question.*

## Matilda

Matilda told such Dreadful Lies,
It made one Gasp and Stretch one's Eyes;
Her Aunt, who, from her Earliest Youth,
Had kept a Strict Regard for Truth,
Attempted to Believe Matilda:
The effort very nearly killed her,
And would have done so, had not She
Discovered this Infirmity.
For once, towards the Close of Day,
Matilda, growing tired of play,
And finding she was left alone,
Went tiptoe to the Telephone
And summoned the Immediate Aid
Of London's Noble Fire-Brigade.
Within an hour the Gallant Band
Were pouring in on every hand,
From Putney, Hackney Downs, and Bow
With Courage high and Hearts a-glow
They galloped, roaring through the Town
'Matilda's House is Burning Down!'

## SAMPLE QUESTION

What do you think the Fire Brigade will find when they get to Matilda's house?

A  a burning house

B  a pile of ashes

C  an intact house

D  a house without any furniture

## STRATEGY

You can guess what might happen next in the poem's narrative by looking for clues in the way it is told. The poet's tone and language choices can provide this insight.

The poet doesn't reveal any sympathy for Matilda. We know Matilda is a liar and that she has summoned the Fire Brigade because she is bored and not because there is a fire. This shows that, when the Fire Brigade arrives 'roaring through the Town' from every corner of London, there will be no fire to put out. She will have caused an extraordinary drama for no reason!

Now look at options **A–D** and decide which best answers the question.

**C is correct.** The house will be intact—exactly as it was when Matilda rang the Fire Brigade.

**A and B are incorrect.** The Fire Brigade will not find a burning house or ashes since there was no fire to begin with.

**D is incorrect.** There is no-one to take the furniture from the house before the Fire Brigade arrives so it will be where it was: inside the house.

# PRACTICE QUESTIONS

*Read this extract from a poem below by Hilaire Belloc then answer the questions.*

## Matilda

It happened that a few Weeks later
Her Aunt was off to the Theatre
To see that Interesting Play
*The Second Mrs Tanqueray*.
She had refused to take her Niece
To hear this Entertaining Piece:
A Deprivation Just and Wise
To Punish her for Telling Lies.
That Night a Fire *did* break out—
You should have heard Matilda Shout!
You should have heard her Scream and Bawl,
And throw the window up and call
To People passing in the Street—
(The rapidly increasing Heat
Encouraging her to obtain
Their confidence) —but all in vain!
For every time She shouted 'Fire!'
They only answered 'Little Liar'!

1 Her Aunt's decision not to take Matilda to the Theatre is
A extremely unfair.
B mean.
C cruel.
D more than reasonable.

2 What will Matilda's Aunt be most likely to find on her return?
A the fire brigade at her house
B neighbours with hoses at her house
C a burnt-down house
D her house just as she left it

☞ **Answers and explanations on page 108**

# Identifying how information and ideas are sequenced

**ACTIVITY:** Sequencing involves putting ideas and information in a logical order. To work out how sentences are connected to each other within a text you need to consider what goes before and after, and how it fits into the whole text.

**SAMPLE QUESTIONS**

*Read the text below then answer the questions.*

Three sentences have been removed from the text. Choose from the sentences (**A–D**) the one which fits each gap (**1–3**). There is one extra sentence which you do not need to use.

## An old emu egg made new

The King Island dwarf emu was hunted into extinction around 1805. **1** _____ French explorers had examples of these birds stuffed and sent back to France for display in museums.

The birds flocked together to gather food (berries, grasses and seaweeds) as well as during breeding time. **2** _____ These eggs were quite big in size as the chicks needed to be born large enough to maintain body heat in the extremely cold climate and to be able to forage for food after hatching.

Recently a very large dwarf emu's egg was found in a sand dune. The finder, Christian Robertson, is a natural historian who lives on King Island and collects emu remains. **3** _____ It has since been found by palaeontologists that this egg could be up to 4000 years old. A fascinating piece of King Island history!

| | |
|---|---|
| A | They generally laid about seven to nine eggs with both parents sharing incubating duties. |
| B | The Tasmanian emu was ten per cent smaller than the mainland variety of emu. |
| C | He pieced the broken pieces of the shell together until he had an almost complete egg. |
| D | It was the smallest of all known emus. |

## Identifying how information and ideas are sequenced

**STRATEGY**

Read the entire passage first so you know what it is about. Read the missing sentences. Find the first space, numbered 1, and think about the subject of its paragraph. Look closely at the sentence before and after the space and work out the sequence of ideas and information. Repeat this procedure for questions 2 and 3.

You need to select the sentence from **A–D** that best connects with these sentences.

1  **D is correct.** The author gives some historical background about the King Island dwarf emu in paragraph one. The sentence before the space tells how and when this bird was made extinct. The missing sentence explains what is distinctive about the bird: It was the smallest of all known emus. The sentence that follows explains how scientists collected and preserved examples of the bird at that time.

2  **A is correct.** The author discusses the birds' behaviour in paragraph two. The sentence before the space refers to feeding and breeding habits. The missing sentence describes the results of their breeding habits: They generally laid about seven to nine eggs with both parents sharing incubating duties. The sentence that follows explains why the eggs the birds laid were large in size.

3  **C is correct.** The author talks about the recent discovery of a large dwarf emu's egg in paragraph three. The sentence before the space tells who found the egg. This missing sentence tells what he did with its broken pieces: He pieced the broken pieces of the shell together until he had an almost complete egg. The sentence that follows reports that its authenticity and approximate age have been verified.

The unused sentence is B.

# PRACTICE QUESTIONS

*Read the text below then answer the questions.*

Three sentences have been removed from the text. Choose from the sentences (**A–D**) the one which fits each gap (**1–3**). There is one extra sentence which you do not need to use.

---

## Mother Teresa

Mary Teresa Bojaxhiu began her life as a Loreto nun. It was the custom to give new nuns a new name. **1** _____ After taking her final vows, her name was changed to Mother Teresa.

Mother Teresa left the convent in 1946 to carry out the mission of devoting her life to caring for the sick and poor. In 1950 she received permission from the Vatican to set up the Missionaries of Charity, an organisation that provided help to those in need. **2** _____ She devoted her whole life to work of this kind and earned the reputation of being saintly in her care of others.

In 1979 the Nobel committee focussed on the sufferings of children and refugees. **3** _____ After her death she was canonised and declared a saint by Pope Francis.

---

| | |
|---|---|
| A | This included orphaned children or those suffering from diseases such as leprosy and AIDS. |
| B | She once said, 'Not all of us can do great things. But we can do small things with great love.' |
| C | The new name she was given, Sister Teresa, paid tribute to that of a saint (Saint Therese de Lisieux). |
| D | It was in this year that Mother Teresa was awarded the Nobel Peace Prize. |

☞ **Answers and explanations on page 108**

# Comparing aspects of texts such as their ideas, forms, structures and language use

**ACTIVITY:** You have to understand what each text is about, its form and how it is written. This will enable you to compare them so you can choose the one that best provides an answer to the question.

## SAMPLE QUESTIONS

*Read the two texts below on the theme of memories.*

For questions **1–3**, choose the option (**A or B**) which you think best answers the question.

Which text …

is about a very unusual 'student'?                                    **1** _____

suggests some memories can be unreliable?                             **2** _____

is about the classroom most different from today?                    **3** _____

---

### TEXT A

Henry Lawson, the poet and short-story writer, recalls the primary school he went to in the 1870s was made of bark and built by his father. It was at a place called Eurunderee in NSW. His father also made blackboards and easels for the students. His teacher was a tall Irishman who camped in a lean-to attached to the school. Lawson remembers 'a great day in my life' was when he was given a copybook, a pen and ink when he started there.

Another memory of his was the black goanna who lived in a dead old tree near the school. It had a habit when it was hot of lying along a beam above the girl's seats. It liked to 'improve his mind a little, and doze a lot'.

---

### TEXT B

I, Pearl Jones, remember most of the names of the children at my first school in Victoria even though it was back in the 1940s, over 70 years ago. There was Christopher Turdish, Gerald Swinnerton and Caroline Blackett. I've never seen them since. We had tiny wooden chairs and if we weren't sitting up straight the teacher would tie rope around our shoulders to keep us upright. I loved school and couldn't bear to miss a day. When our work was all correct, we could choose an animal stamp as a reward. The little purple inky stamp smudged easily on your page. I usually chose the rhinoceros.

Later when I went to Uni I met one of my friends called Robert Easterly from that school. He told me I had chased him all around the playground with a needle and thread when he tore his trousers on a tree branch. I can't remember that at all!

---

# Comparing aspects of texts such as their ideas, forms, structures and language use

## STRATEGY

When finding which text offers the answer to a question you need to have a good grasp of what each text is about and how it is written.

The author of Text A tells us about Henry Lawson's memories of his time at a bush school back in the 1870s. His school experiences are unusual and describe a classroom unfamiliar to a modern audience. This account of Lawson's memories includes some quotations of things he actually said when recalling his time at his school in the bush.

Text B is a first-person record of Pearl Jones's memories of attending school in the 1940s. She recalls unconnected details about her early time at school: the names of the students, a discipline practice and the rewards you could get for good work. She then switches to a later time frame which gives her another perspective on her early days at school. Could she have forgotten some details?

Now look at the questions and decide which text best answers the questions.

1 **A is correct.** Text A quotes Henry Lawson as saying the goanna liked to 'improve his mind' when he was lying along a beam in the roof of the classroom above the girls' seats. He is jokingly implying the goanna was occasionally a scholar along with the other students. A goanna is certainly an unusual type of scholar! (The students in Pearl's classroom in Text B are not unusual in any way.)

2 **B is correct.** Text B refers to Pearl meeting up with a classmate, Robert, when they are at university. His memory of an event that happened at their school is one that Pearl can't recall. Whose memory is accurate? Pearl doesn't know the answer to this question, which raises the idea that memory may sometimes be unreliable. (Doubts about memories being inaccurate are not raised in Text A.)

3 **A is correct.** Both Text A and Text B recall classrooms that have recognisable differences from a modern classroom. However, you can judge that Text A records many more differences than Text B. These include having your father build the school and some of its equipment, having the teacher living in a lean-to beside the classroom, using a copy book with a pen and ink, and allowing a goanna in the classroom. Text B only records one main difference: the discipline of tying children to their seats to improve their posture. You would be unlikely to find this in a modern classroom. Animal stamps is another possible difference but they are still given as rewards in some modern classrooms.

# PRACTICE QUESTIONS

*Read the two texts below on the theme of memories.*

For questions **1–3**, choose the option (**A or B**) which you think best answers the question.

Which text …

is made up mainly of personal memories?

**1** _____

includes quotations from a well-known author?

**2** _____

describes a form of discipline now out of favour?

**3** _____

---

**TEXT A**

Henry Lawson, the poet and short-story writer, recalls the primary school he went to in the 1870s was made of bark and built by his father. It was at a place called Eurunderee in NSW. His father also made blackboards and easels for the students. His teacher was a tall Irishman who camped in a lean-to attached to the school. Lawson remembers 'a great day in my life' was when he was given a copybook, a pen and ink when he started there.

Another memory of his was the black goanna who lived in a dead old tree near the school. It had a habit when it was hot of lying along a beam above the girl's seats. It liked to 'improve his mind a little, and doze a lot'.

---

**TEXT B**

I, Pearl Jones, remember most of the names of the children at my first school in Victoria even though it was back in the 1940s, over 70 years ago. There was Christopher Turdish, Gerald Swinnerton and Caroline Blackett. I've never seen them since. We had tiny wooden chairs and if we weren't sitting up straight the teacher would tie rope around our shoulders to keep us upright. I loved school and couldn't bear to miss a day. When our work was all correct, we could choose an animal stamp as a reward. The little purple inky stamp smudged easily on your page. I usually chose the rhinoceros.

Later when I went to Uni I met one of my friends called Robert Easterly from that school. He told me I had chased him all around the playground with a needle and thread when he tore his trousers on a tree branch. I can't remember that at all!

---

☞ **Answers and explanations on page 109**

# Drawing a conclusion

**ACTIVITY:** You need to evaluate the evidence presented in an argument. A correct conclusion must be supported by evidence. A conclusion is not possible or cannot be true if the evidence does not support it.

**SAMPLE QUESTION 1**

Aida's school was preparing for the election of the Student Leadership Team. Before the vote could take place, candidates had to be selected. Potential candidates could be nominated by a teacher or they could nominate themselves. They then had to complete a community-service challenge as well as an interview with the selection committee and the Principal.

If a student was nominated by a teacher, they only had to pass the community-service challenge in order to be selected as a candidate. If a student was not nominated by a teacher, they either needed an excellent result in the community-service challenge or they needed to do well in both the community-service challenge and the interview.

Aida was nominated by a teacher but failed to be selected as a candidate for the election.

Based on the above information, which one of the following statements must be true?

A  Aida did badly in the interview.

B  Aida was not nominated by a teacher.

C  Aida did well in the community-service challenge but badly in the interview.

D  Aida failed the community-service challenge.

## STRATEGY

1  Read the information in the box.

2  Read the question.

3  To answer this question you need to identify whether a conclusion that is not stated can be drawn from the information provided.

4  Read each statement in turn and evaluate if it must be true. Remember: There could be a trick, such as the inclusion of a statement that might be true. Unless the statement must be true, it is not the correct answer.

**D is correct.** Since Aida was nominated by a teacher, the result of the interview was not relevant in her case. She only had to pass the community-service challenge to be selected as a candidate for the election. Since she was not selected as a candidate, she must have failed the community-service challenge. So this statement **must** be true.

**A is incorrect.** This statement **might** be true. However, since Aida was nominated by a teacher, the result of the interview was not relevant in her case. She only had to pass the community-service challenge to be selected as a candidate for the election. So, based on the information provided, we cannot say this statement **must** be true.

**B is incorrect.** The question tells us Aida was nominated by a teacher.

**C is incorrect.** Since Aida was nominated by a teacher, she only had to pass the community-service challenge to be selected as a candidate for the election. So the statement that she did well in the challenge cannot be true since Aida failed to be selected.

## *Drawing a conclusion*

**SAMPLE QUESTION 2**

**Wei:** 'Let's go to the mall after school.'

**Tom:** 'No, I can't. I have to study for the Maths test tomorrow. If I don't study, I will likely fail.'

**Wei:** 'And if you fail the test, your parents won't be happy!'

**Tom:** 'Yes! If they are happy, they might let me go to the concert next weekend. Otherwise there is no way they will agree.'

Based on the above information, which one of the following statements **cannot** be true?

A  Tom did not study but his parents said yes to the concert.

B  Tom studied but his parents did not let him go to the concert.

C  Tom's parents were unhappy with him but they let him go to the concert.

D  Tom's parents were happy with him but they did not say yes to the concert.

**STRATEGY**

1  Read the information in the box.

2  Read the question.

3  To answer this question, you need to identify whether a conclusion is impossible based on the information provided.

4  Read each statement in turn and evaluate whether it cannot be true. Remember: There could be a statement that might or might not be true. However, unless the statement cannot be true, it is not the correct answer.

**C is correct.** From the information provided, you can draw the conclusion that if Tom's parents are unhappy with him, there is no way they will let him go to the concert. So this conclusion **cannot** be true.

**A is incorrect**. This statement **might** be true. Even though Tom did not study, he could still have passed the test and made his parents happy. And if they were happy, they may have let him go to the concert.

**B is incorrect**. This statement **might** be true. Tom might have studied but still failed the Maths test. Or he might have studied and passed the test but his parents still didn't let him go to the concert.

**D is incorrect**. This statement **might** be true. The information tells us that if Tom's parents are happy with him, they might let him go to the concert—not that they will definitely let him go to the concert.

# Identifying an assumption

**ACTIVITY:** You need to evaluate the evidence and the conclusion drawn from that evidence to work out any assumptions made in reaching this conclusion. Note that it is easy to make assumptions that lead to incorrect conclusions.

## SAMPLE QUESTION 1

Chloe is in the kitchen making a pavlova when her friend Suma arrives.

**Suma:** 'You love making pavlova!'

**Chloe:** 'No, I hate it! It's hard work beating egg whites. It takes forever!'

**Suma:** 'Why are you making one, then?'

**Chloe:** 'It's Dad's birthday. And pavlova is his favourite dessert.'

Which assumption has Suma made in order to draw her conclusion?

A  Everyone loves eating pavlova.

B  Chloe's father loves eating pavlova.

C  Everyone who makes a pavlova loves making pavlova.

D  Everyone knows beating egg whites for pavlova takes forever.

## STRATEGY

1  Read the dialogue between Suma and Chloe.

2  Read the question.

3  To answer this question you need to identify an assumption that has been made in order to draw a conclusion. Remember: An assumption is not stated in a text. Instead it is something that is taken for granted.

4  Ask yourself what Suma's conclusion is. What is the main point she is trying to get you to accept? (Chloe loves making pavlova.)

5  Now ask yourself what evidence she has based this conclusion on. (Chloe is making a pavlova.)

6  Read and think about each statement listed. Which one of the statements would you need to take for granted to draw the conclusion that Suma drew?

**C is correct**. For Suma's conclusion to hold, it must be assumed that everyone who makes a pavlova loves making pavlova. (Chloe is making a pavlova + everyone who makes a pavlova loves making pavlova means therefore Chloe loves making pavlova.)

**A is incorrect**. This assumption does not support Suma's conclusion that Chloe loves making pavlova. (Chloe is making a pavlova + everyone loves eating pavlova **does not mean** therefore Chloe loves making pavlova.)

**B is incorrect**. This is the real reason why Chloe is making a pavlova, not the assumption that Suma made.

**D is incorrect**. This assumption does not support Suma's conclusion. She would need to also assume that Chloe loves doing hard things that take forever to reach the conclusion that Chloe loves making pavlova.

## *Identifying an assumption*

**SAMPLE QUESTION 2**

A dog trainer was speaking on television about different methods of training dogs.

**Dog trainer:** 'We should not use cruel methods to train dogs. Therefore we should not use choke collars on dogs.'

Which assumption has the dog trainer made in order to draw his conclusion?

A   Choke collars are cruel.

B   Choke collars should not be used on dogs.

C   Dogs do not respond well to cruel training methods.

D   All dog trainers use choke collars.

### STRATEGY

1   Read the information in the box.

2   Read the question.

3   To answer this question you need to identify an assumption that has been made in order to draw a conclusion. Remember: An assumption is not stated in a text; Instead it is something taken for granted.

4   Ask yourself what the dog trainer's conclusion is. What is the main point that he is trying to get you to accept? (We should not use choke collars on dogs.)

Now ask yourself what evidence he has based this conclusion on. (We should not use cruel methods to train dogs.)

Read and think about each statement listed. Which one of those statements would you need to take for granted in order to draw the conclusion that the dog trainer drew?

**A is correct.** For the dog trainer's conclusion to hold, it must be assumed that choke collars are cruel. (We should not use cruel methods to train dogs + choke collars are cruel means therefore we should not use choke collars on dogs.)

**B is incorrect.** This is the dog trainer's conclusion, not his assumption.

**C is incorrect.** This assumption does not support the dog trainer's conclusion that we should not use choke collars on dogs. (We should not use cruel methods to train dogs + dogs do not respond well to cruel training methods **does not mean** therefore we should not use choke collars on dogs.) The trainer would still also need to assume that choke collars are cruel.

**D is incorrect.** This assumption does not support the dog trainer's conclusion that we should not use choke collars on dogs. (We should not use cruel methods to train dogs + all dog trainers use choke collars **does not mean** therefore we should not use choke collars on dogs.)

# Assessing the impact of additional evidence

**ACTIVITY:** You need to evaluate a claim or argument and judge whether additional evidence will weaken or strengthen that argument.

## SAMPLE QUESTION 1

> The Oldtown Council was meeting to consider closing the local public garden. Mrs Nargundkar, one of the gardeners, spoke at the meeting.

**Mrs Nargundkar:** 'We must keep our Oldtown Public Garden open. It is a much-loved public space and provides solace and joy to many people in the area. Not only does the garden evoke beauty and inspiration, but it is also important for the mental health of our community.'

Which one of these statements, if true, most **strengthens** Mrs Nargundkar's argument?

A  Research shows that green spaces play an important role in connecting people.

B  A developer wants to use the land to build a shopping mall.

C  If the Garden closes, the gardeners employed there might find it difficult to get work.

D  People who visit the Oldtown Garden are always happy.

### STRATEGY

1  Read the text.

2  Read the question.

3  Work out what argument Mrs Nargundkar is making in her speech to the meeting. (She is arguing that the Council should keep the Old Town Garden open because of its importance to the community.)

4  Decide what additional information would most strengthen this argument.

5  Consider the answer options. You need to find the statement that most shows the importance to the community of the Garden.

**A is correct.** If research shows that green spaces play an important role in connecting people, this will strengthen the argument that the garden is important to the community. Remember to check the other answer options to ensure you have chosen the correct answer that **most** strengthens the argument.

**B is incorrect.** This statement provides extra information about why the Council is considering closing the garden but it does not strengthen Mrs Nargundkar's argument about the importance of the garden to the community.

**C is incorrect.** This statement provides extra information about a possible impact of closing the garden. It could be used in an argument against closing the garden but it does not strengthen Mrs Nargundkar's argument about the importance of the garden to the community.

**D is incorrect.** This is a restatement of a comment Mrs Nargundkar has already made — that the garden 'provides solace and joy to many people' — so it doesn't strengthen the argument.

## Assessing the impact of additional evidence

**SAMPLE QUESTION 2**

> Arshan's mum and dad are deciding what to do for their next holiday.

**Mum:** 'Work is so busy this year. Let's just book a group tour. Then we don't have to think about anything. We can just pack our bags and go.'

**Dad:** 'A group tour would be really boring. We'd have to spend all day travelling on a bus, only getting off at crowded attractions, having a quick look around and then getting right back on the bus again. I don't want to sit on a bus all day.'

Which one of these statements, if true, most **weakens** Dad's argument?

A  A group tour is convenient.

B  Tour groups save time by not having to queue.

C  Most group tours travel by bus.

D  Some group tours are trekking or cycling trips.

**STRATEGY**

1  Read the text.

2  Read the question.

3  Identify the argument Dad is making. (He is arguing that a group tour would be boring because they'd have to sit on a bus all day.)

4  Decide what additional information would most weaken the argument.

5  Consider the answer options. You need to find the statement that best shows a group tour is not boring and they won't have to sit on a bus all day.

**D is correct.** On a trekking or cycling group tour they would spend the day walking or cycling rather than sitting on a bus. So this statement weakens Dad's argument that a group tour would be boring and they'd sit on a bus all day.

**A is incorrect.** This statement supports Mum's argument about not having to think of anything on a group tour. However, it does not weaken Dad's argument about sitting on a bus all day.

**B is incorrect.** This statement could strengthen an argument in favour of going on a group tour but it does not weaken Dad's argument about sitting on a bus all day.

**C is incorrect.** This statement supports Dad's argument about sitting on a bus all day. It does not weaken it.

# Checking reasoning to detect errors

**ACTIVITY:** You need to analyse the reasoning used in an argument or claim. If the reasoning holds up, the claim might be accepted. If the reasoning does not make sense or is flawed, the claim or argument can be rejected.

**SAMPLE QUESTION 1**

> Whenever the yellow light on the battery charger flashes off and on it means the battery is charging.

**Cameron:** 'The yellow light is on continuously. The battery must be completely charged.'

**Mari:** 'No, if a flashing yellow light means the battery is charging, a yellow light that isn't flashing must mean the battery is dead.'

If the information in the box is true, whose reasoning is correct?

**A** Cameron

**B** Mari

**C** Both Cameron and Mari

**D** Neither Cameron nor Mari

## STRATEGY

1  Read the question. You need to detect any errors in reasoning made by Cameron or Mari.

2  Read the information in the box.

3  Read and think about each child's argument. Check each argument for any flaws or mistakes. Has the child made a mistake or not thought of something?

4  Remember: One child's reasoning might be correct, both children's reasoning might be correct or neither child's reasoning might be correct. So do not settle on an answer until you have checked each child's argument for flaws.

**D is correct.** Neither Cameron's nor Mari's reasoning is correct.

**A is incorrect.** Cameron's reasoning that the battery must be completely charged has a flaw. No information is given about the meaning of a yellow light that is on continuously. For example, the light might be broken so that it no longer flashes or a different-coloured light might indicate a full charge.

**B is incorrect.** Mari's reasoning is also flawed, since no information is given about the meaning of a yellow light that is not flashing. She cannot say with certainty that it **must** mean the battery is dead.

**C is incorrect.** Both Cameron's and Mari's reasoning is flawed.

## *Checking reasoning to detect errors*

**SAMPLE QUESTION 2**

> David's mother entered a pumpkin in the best vegetable contest at the local community fair. In the contest each gardener is allowed to enter only one vegetable. Judges score all entries. Ribbons are then awarded for first, second and third, and a special ribbon to anyone who has entered the contest for three consecutive years.

**David:** 'This year there is only one gardener who has entered for three consecutive years. So that means four gardeners will get ribbons.'

Which one of the following sentences shows the mistake David has made?

A One gardener might be awarded a ribbon for more than one vegetable.

B The gardener who entered for three consecutive years might have come first, second or third.

C Some gardeners might deserve a prize if they missed last year but entered for the two consecutive years before that.

D We don't know how many gardeners entered the contest.

### STRATEGY

1 Read the information in the box and David's conclusion.

2 Read the question. It tells you that David's reasoning is flawed. You must now identify the flaw by working out a mistake he has made or something he has not thought of.

3 Read and think about each sentence. Does its show the mistake David made?

Remember, a sentence might show a mistake or a flaw in reasoning. But it might not be the mistake that David made. You must find the sentence that shows David's mistake.

**B is correct.** This sentence shows the mistake David has made. To come to the conclusion that four gardeners will get ribbons, David has added the one ribbon for entering for three consecutive years to the ribbons awarded for first, second and third. He has not thought that the gardener who entered for the third consecutive year might also have come first, second or third—and therefore will receive two of the ribbons, meaning only three gardeners might get ribbons.

**A is incorrect.** The information tells us each gardener can only enter one item, which is a mistake. However, it is not a mistake David has made.

**C is incorrect.** The information tells us that to get the special ribbon a gardener must have entered for three consecutive years. So this sentence shows a mistake in reasoning. However, it is not a mistake David has made.

**D is incorrect.** This sentence is true but does not affect the number of ribbons awarded. It is also not a mistake David has made.

# PRACTICE QUESTIONS

**1** Shops and offices at the intersection of Sydney Road and Melbourne Street could be bulldozed to make way for a ten-story block of premium apartments. The building under threat has been standing for over 100 years and is an important part of the history of the local area and the character of the streetscape. We urge planning authorities to refuse the development application.

Which one of the following, if true, most **strengthens** the above argument?

A The area is in urgent need of more basic housing for low-income workers.

B The proposed development will include four new retail outlets.

C A heritage report has stated that the building is the last remaining example of inter-war architecture in the area.

D The building height will overshadow the community plaza.

**2**

The school principal is addressing the debating club before the Schools Debating Championship finals.

**Principal:** 'If we don't win this debate, it will hurt the reputation of the school. So we must win this debate!'

Which assumption has the principal made in order to draw her conclusion?

A The school team must win the debate.

B The school debate team is not very strong.

C Students at the school get excited when their team wins.

D Students must not do anything to hurt the reputation of the school.

☞ Answers and explanations on pages 109–110

## Practice questions

**3**

Grace's teacher told the class that any students who did not get a chance to work in the kitchen garden last term will definitely be selected to work in the garden this term.

**Grace:** 'Oh no, I worked in the kitchen garden last term. That means I won't be allowed to work there this term. I loved working in the garden!'

Which one of the following sentences shows the mistake Grace has made?

A  Just because anyone who didn't get a chance to work in the garden last term will be selected to work there this term, it doesn't mean anyone who worked there last term will not be selected to work there again this term.

B  Just because someone didn't get a chance to work in the garden last term, it doesn't mean they would not have liked to work in the garden.

C  Just because Grace worked in the garden last term, it does not mean she will be selected to work there this term.

D  Just because someone didn't get a chance to work in the garden last term, it doesn't mean they will be selected to work in the garden this term.

**4**  The kitchen garden committee was discussing ideas to raise funds to buy new compost bins. They found that anyone who was in favour of selling eggs from the hens was also in favour of a raffle. They also found that anyone in favour of a raffle was in favour of a quiz night but no-one in favour of a raffle was in favour of creating a book of favourite recipes using produce from the garden.

On the basis of this information, which conclusion must be true?

A  If Joe is not in favour of creating a recipe book, he does not want a quiz night.

B  If Liora is in favour of selling eggs, she does not want to create a recipe book.

C  If Yitong is not in favour of selling eggs, she does not want a quiz night.

D  If Kinta is in favour of a quiz night, he is also in favour of a raffle.

☞ **Answers and explanations on pages 109–110**

# Spatial reasoning

**ACTIVITY:** The requirement for this kind of reasoning is visuo-spatial skill. Not only must the student be able to identify key parts of a pattern within a figure and manipulate these parts within their mind but this ability must be further projected into the area of three-dimensional shapes.

Questions on space are very common in both Selective Schools and Scholarship Tests.

## SAMPLE QUESTION 1

The four pieces shown below can be placed in the square to complete this puzzle. (They might need to be rotated to fit.)

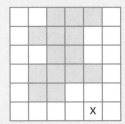

Which of the four pieces will cover the square marked by the **X**?

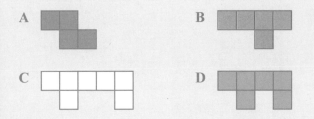

A       B

C       D

### STRATEGY

In your mind you must place the pieces from the options into the square. You need to find the piece that covers the X. In doing this it might be easier to begin somewhere else in the square.

The only piece that can be placed on the top on the left side is the piece in option D. Once that piece is in place, the only piece that can then fit on the bottom left is the piece in option C and it will cover the square marked X.

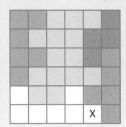

The correct answer is C.

## SAMPLE QUESTION 2

How many edges, faces and vertices in total will the solid have when it has been formed from this net?

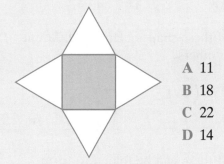

A  11
B  18
C  22
D  14

### STRATEGY

Not having the actual shape in front of you, it must be manipulated in your head. This is a fairly simple form of question to start off with. You will quickly form the square pyramid in your head and it is simply then just a matter of counting, again in your head. (Sometimes closing your eyes can help you concentrate better on this kind of problem.) The faces will be 5 (the square and the four triangles); the edges will total 8 (4 where the triangular sides meet the square base and 4 where each triangle meets the other triangles— don't count all the sides of all the triangles or you'll end up with answer C which is wrong); the vertices will total 5 (the point at the top and the 4 around the angles of the square). This gives a total of 18. **The correct answer is B.**

# PRACTICE QUESTIONS

**1** In these four shapes, two have the same pattern except that one of the two has been rotated through 180°. Which two?

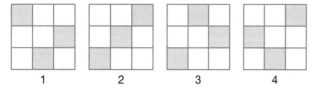

1      2      3      4

**A** 1 and 2    **B** 1 and 3
**C** 3 and 4    **D** 2 and 4

**2** Which of these shapes below is different from the others?

A      B      C      D

**3** Which of these can be folded to form a cube?

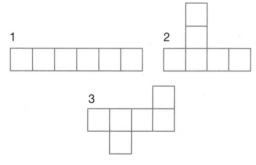

**A** 1 only      **B** 2 only
**C** 3 only      **D** 2 and 3 only

**4** Helena has these four shapes, two of which are exactly the same.

How many of the following shapes can be made using Helena's four shapes? (They can be turned over or around.)

**A** 1    **B** 2    **C** 3    **D** 4

**5** These shapes are four pieces of a puzzle. When completed the puzzle is a square.

Which could be the remaining piece?

A            B

C            D

Answers and explanations on page 110

# Logical reasoning

**ACTIVITY:** This type of reasoning uses clear thinking and common sense. It might involve placing people or objects in order or determining which of a set of statements must be true or might not be true. It is very important to read the question carefully and take time to think about what is required.

## SAMPLE QUESTION 1

Alexander, Harrison, Isabella, Jill, Oliver and Rebecca are siblings.

- Rebecca and Isabella are twins.
- Harrison is 7.
- Oliver is older than Jill but younger than Alexander.
- Harrison is older than Isabella but younger than Oliver.

Which of the following statements must be true?

A  Oliver is 8.

B  Jill is the youngest.

C  Alexander is the oldest

D  Rebecca is older than Harrison.

## STRATEGY

Read the question carefully and take note of what is required. Here we are looking for the statement that must be true. This doesn't mean the other statements will necessarily be false. We need to consider each option.

**A might be true**. Oliver is older than Harrison and Harrison is 7. So Oliver might be 8 but he might also be older than 8.

**B might be true**. Jill is younger than Oliver, who is younger than Alexander, but she might be older than Rebecca and Isabella or Harrison.

**C is true**. Alexander is older than Oliver, who is older than both Harrison and Jill. Harrison is older than both Rebecca and Isabella. So Alexander must be the oldest.

**D is not true**. Harrison is older than Isabella, and Rebecca and Isabella are the same age so Harrison must be older than Rebecca. **The correct answer is C**.

## SAMPLE QUESTION 2

| Villa Street | 1 | 2 | 3 | 4 | 5 |
|---|---|---|---|---|---|
| | | | | | |

Five men—Alf, David, Jim, Russell and Sergei— live in five villas all in a row. Villa 1 is at the front, closest to the road, and villa 5 is at the back of the row.

- Alf is not in villa 1.
- Jim is somewhere between Alf and David.
- Sergei's villa is further towards the back than Russell's and there are exactly two villas between them.
- David's villa has a higher number than at least two others.

Who is in villa 2?

A  Alf                   B  Jim

C  Russell              D  Sergei

## STRATEGY

In this type of question the answer is not immediately obvious. So we work through the given information, organising what we can. In this way some options can be eliminated and the order gradually falls into place.

Here we are told that Alf is not in villa 1. David is not in villa 1 because his villa number must be at least 3. Jim is not in villa 1 because he is between Alf and David. Sergei is not in villa 1 because he is further back than Russell. So Russell must be in villa 1.

As there are exactly two villas between Russell and Sergei, Sergei must be in villa 4. Jim is between Alf and David so must be in 3. So Alf must be in 2 and David in 5. **The correct answer is A**.

| Villa Street | 1 | 2 | 3 | 4 | 5 |
|---|---|---|---|---|---|
| | Russell | Alf | Jim | Sergei | David |

# PRACTICE QUESTIONS

**1** Five businesses are in a row on the northern side of a street.

- The bank is somewhere west of the post office and somewhere east of the real-estate office.
- The chemist is next to the newsagency.
- The newsagency is somewhere east of, but not next to, the bank.
- There are two businesses between the real-estate office and the chemist.

Which business is in the middle of the row?

A bank
B chemist
C newsagency
D post office

**2** Five boys competed in a hurdles race.

- Dean didn't knock over any hurdles but finished last.
- Grant was faster than Jonathan but knocked over two hurdles.
- Pedro knocked over more hurdles than Grant but finished before him.
- Isaac knocked over fewer hurdles than Pedro but finished after him.
- Jonathan knocked over the same number of hurdles as Isaac but wasn't as fast.

Which one of the following statements cannot be true?

A Pedro did not finish first.
B Isaac knocked over one hurdle.
C Jonathan finished in fourth place.
D Grant knocked over fewer hurdles than Jonathan.

**3** Six friends—Oliver, Cooper, Wendy, Sonia, Arden and Imogen—lined up in a queue. Wendy and Cooper were next to each other. Oliver was second. Arden was two places after Sonia. Imogen was in front of Cooper but behind Sonia. Which of the following must be true?

A Sonia was third.
B Imogen was fourth.
C Wendy was behind Cooper.
D Oliver was four places in front of Cooper.

**4** Six boys—Felix, Jhye, Knox, Rowan, Silas and Theo—and six girls—Aurelia, Esme, Millie, Ophelia, Rose and Willow—live in Kintyre Close.

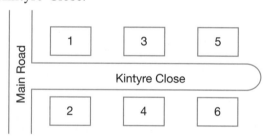

- Three of the boys are brothers who live at No. 3.
- Millie and Willow live next door to each other. They both have one brother but no sisters.
- Best friends Rose and Ophelia live at opposite ends of the Close and on opposite sides of the road. Rose has no siblings.
- Esme and her brother Theo live directly across the road from Ophelia.
- Aurelia and her sister live next door to Willow.
- Theo's house number is higher than Rose's.

At what number house does Millie live?
A 2    B 4    C 5    D 6

☞ **Answers and explanations on pages 110–111**

# Solving problems

**ACTIVITY:** Some questions do not follow a particular pattern but might be quite unusual or different to what has been seen before. They test a student's ability to process information and solve problems. It is important to read the question carefully and understand what is required. Although there is not much time to waste in these tests, taking time to think is not a waste and may actually save you time in the long run and prevent lots of unnecessary work.

## SAMPLE QUESTION 1

Imran, Ivy and Cameron are playing a game. They each begin with 25 points and take it in turns to roll a dice. Points are allocated according to this table.

| Roll | Action |
|------|--------|
| 1 | Give 1 point to each of the others. |
| 2 | Give 2 points to each of the others. |
| 3 | Give 3 points to each of the others. |
| 4 | Receive 1 point from each of the others. |
| 5 | Receive 2 points from each of the others. |
| 6 | Receive 3 points from each of the others. |

After the first round, each person having rolled the dice once, Imran has 32 points. In that first round Imran rolled a 6 and Ivy rolled a 2.

How many points does Cameron have at the end of the first round?

**A** 23    **B** 24    **C** 25    **D** 26

### STRATEGY

Read the question carefully and make sure that you understand, firstly, the rules of the game. Then work through the game as it would be played.

Imran began with 25 points. Rolling a 6, he would have received 3 points from Ivy and 3 points from Cameron. He would then have 31 points and Ivy and Cameron would both have 22 points.

Ivy rolled a 2 so would need to give 2 points to Imran and 2 to Cameron. Imran would have 33 points, Ivy 18 points and Cameron 24 points.

After Cameron's roll, Imran has 32 points so he must have given one point to Cameron. Ivy must have also given one point to Cameron so he would have 26 points. **The correct answer is D.**

## SAMPLE QUESTION 2

Toby has been rolling a normal dice and adding the result each time. From four rolls of the dice he has a total of 12. Three rolls of the dice showed the same number but the other was a different number. What was that different number?

**A** 2    **B** 3    **C** 5    **D** 6

### STRATEGY

Read the question carefully and determine the important points. A dice has been rolled four times, with the same number coming up three of the four times. The total of all the rolls was 12.

As $3 \times 4 = 12$, the number that was rolled three times must have been less than 4.

If the same number was 3, the other number would also have to be 3 to add up to 12. As, the other number must be different, this cannot be the case.

If the same number was 2, as $3 \times 2 = 6$, the other number would have to be 6 to add to 12.

If the same number was 1, as $3 \times 1 = 3$, the other number would have to be 9 and, as a number from the roll of a dice cannot be more than 6, this cannot be the case.

So the first number had to be 2 and the different number had to be 6. **The correct answer is D.**

# PRACTICE QUESTIONS

**1** There are seven competitors in a competition where each one will receive a minimum of 3 and a maximum of 10 points in each round. In any round, no two competitors can receive the same number of points. The results for the first four rounds are shown in the table.

| Name | Round 1 | Round 2 | Round 3 | Round 4 |
|------|---------|---------|---------|---------|
| Oscar | 7 | 10 | 9 | 3 |
| Sonia | 9 | 3 | 5 | 7 |
| Abdul | 10 | 8 | 6 | 9 |
| Zac | 6 | 7 | 4 | 10 |
| Ruby | 4 | 5 | 8 | 5 |
| Elise | 5 | 6 | 10 | 8 |
| Ricky | 8 | 9 | 7 | 6 |

One competitor will definitely win the competition outright if they score enough points in the fifth and final round. What is the minimum score the competitor can get to be guaranteed the win?

A 6        B 7        C 8        D 9

**2** There are 43 houses in Edith Street and a total of 68 cars that are normally garaged at those houses. Four houses have three cars garaged at them, which is the most at any address, and every house has at least one car.

How many houses have exactly one car garaged at that address?

A 17        B 21        C 22        D 26

**3** Cheryl, Gian, Tony and Sophia are standing beside each other for a photo. In how many different positions could they stand facing the camera?

A 12        B 20        C 24        D 10

**4** These facts are known about five children.

Lachlan is younger than Veronica but not as tall as Nathan.

Zoe is younger than Ronald but taller than Veronica.

Veronica is taller than Ronald but shorter than Lachlan.

Which one of these statements **cannot** be true?

A Nathan is the tallest.
B Zoe is the tallest.
C Ronald is both the oldest and shortest.
D Veronica is not the second shortest.

**5** If you begin with a one-digit integer (1–9), multiply it by 3, add 8, divide by 2 and subtract 6, you will get the integer back. What number is it?

A 2        B 4        C 6        D 8

**6** Kelly has a friend who lives overseas. Kelly knows the phone number for her friend has seven digits after the number code for the country. She also knows a few other things.

- Every one of the seven digits is different.
- The last digit is 7.
- The two-digit number formed by the first two numbers is twice that of the two-digit number formed by the last two numbers.
- The two-digit number formed by the first two numbers is half of the three-digit number formed by the middle three digits.

What is the middle digit of the seven-digit number?

A 0        B 1        C 2        D 4

☞ **Answers and explanations on page 111**

# Numerical reasoning

**ACTIVITY:** Many questions require use of simple numerical rules and processes. They might, for example, involve basic arithmetic or use of fractions. Questions test students' understanding of these processes but, in general, do not require complicated manipulation. It is more a case of using common sense and applying basic numerical knowledge.

## SAMPLE QUESTION 1

Jody, Frank and Anna all round the number 7 642 398. Jody rounds it to the nearest hundred, Frank rounds it to the nearest thousand and Anna rounds it to the nearest hundred thousand.

Which statement is correct?

A Jody's answer is the smallest and Anna's is the largest.

B Frank's answer is the smallest and Anna's is the largest.

C Jody's answer is the smallest and Frank's answer is the largest.

D Anna's answer is the smallest and Jody's is the largest.

E Anna's answer is the smallest and Frank's is the largest.

## STRATEGY

Read the question carefully, including the options, and think about what is required. We basically need to determine whose answer will be the smallest and whose will be the largest when the number is rounded off in the stated way.

Jody rounded 7 642 398 to the nearest hundred. Her answer will be 7 642 400 because 398 is between 300 and 400 and closer to 400 than 300. We can ignore the first part of the number when we work out the rounding, but, of course, cannot ignore that part of the number in the answer.

Frank rounded 7 642 398 to the nearest thousand. His answer will be 7 642 000 because 2398 is between 2000 and 3000 and closer to 2000.

Anna rounded 7 642 398 to the nearest hundred thousand. Her answer will be 7 600 000 because 642 398 is closer to 600 000 than to 700 000.

Now compare their answers: 7 642 400, 7 642 000 and 7 600 000. Anna's answer is the smallest and Jody's is the largest. **The correct answer is D.**

## SAMPLE QUESTION 2

Joe made 10 lamingtons and ate three of them. Pia ate $\frac{1}{5}$ of the amount Joe made.

Which of the following statements are correct?

X Joe ate more than a quarter of the lamingtons.

Y Pia ate less than a quarter of the lamingtons.

Z Together Joe and Pia ate half of the lamingtons.

A X only

B X and Y only

C X and Z only

D Y and Z only

E X, Y and Z

## STRATEGY

Read the question carefully. Here we need to determine whether or not three different statements are correct so each needs to be considered separately. First we need to determine how many lamingtons each person ate. We are told that Joe ate 3 out of 10 and Pia ate $\frac{1}{5}$ of 10. As $10 \div 5 = 2$, Pia must have eaten 2 of the 10 lamingtons. Now, one-half of 10 is 5 and a quarter of 10 is half of 5 or $2\frac{1}{2}$. So statement X is correct: Joe ate more than a quarter of the lamingtons. Statement Y is also correct: Pia ate less than a quarter. Together Joe and Pia ate 5 so statement Z is also correct. **The correct answer is E.**

# PRACTICE QUESTIONS

**1** Nell puts 10 beads on a string. There are two red beads, $\frac{3}{5}$ of the beads are blue and the rest are white.

How many beads are white?

| 1 | 2 | 3 | 4 | 5 |
|---|---|---|---|---|
| A | B | C | D | E |

**2** △ and ☐ represent two different numbers. Each symbol represents the same number each time it appears.

△ × 8 = 72    and

☐ + ☐ + △ + △ + △ = 37

What number does ☐ represent?

| 4 | 5 | 6 | 7 | 8 |
|---|---|---|---|---|
| A | B | C | D | E |

**3** Sam adds the smallest three-digit whole number to the largest four-digit whole number. What should his answer be?

| 10 099 | 10 999 | 10 100 | 11 000 | 10 090 |
|---|---|---|---|---|
| A | B | C | D | E |

**4** In the number 95 324 the value of the digit 2 is 20. How many times larger is the value of the digit 9 than that of the digit 3?

| 30 | 60 | 100 | 300 | 600 |
|---|---|---|---|---|
| A | B | C | D | E |

**5** Brooke counted the whole numbers between 1 and 99 that were multiples of 5 and multiples of 2.

She made these statements:
X There are 20 multiples of 5.
Y There are 50 multiples of 2.
Z There are 9 multiples of both 2 and 5.

Which statements are correct?

A X only
B Y only
C Z only
D X and Y only
E X, Y and Z

**6** Five children—Geri, Danny, Nadia, Vinh and Ruby—collected cards. All the children collected a different number of cards, the most being 12. Danny collected 11 cards and Ruby collected 8, which was the least. Geri collected more than Vinh but less than Nadia. Which must be true?

A Danny collected more than Nadia.
B Nadia collected one more than Geri.
C Geri collected one more than Vinh.
D Ruby collected three less than Nadia.
E Vinh collected one less than Danny.

**7** Every row, every column and both diagonals of this magic square add to the same amount. What number should go where the X is?

|   |   |   |
|---|---|---|
| 4 |   |   |
| 3 | 5 |   |
|   | 1 | X |

| 7 | 9 | 6 | 8 | 2 |
|---|---|---|---|---|
| A | B | C | D | E |

☞ **Answers and explanations on pages 111–112**

# Working with measurements

**ACTIVITY:** Familiarity with basic units of measurement is important. The prefixes centi, milli and kilo should be understood, as they apply to many different measurements, including measurements of length, mass (weight) and capacity. You must be able to read measuring instruments. It is also important to understand that units of time are different and be able to work with seconds, minutes and hours as well as 12- and 24-hour time and with calendars.

## SAMPLE QUESTION 1

Lizzie has this jug of juice. She pours juice from the jug to fill six glasses that each hold 250 mL. Immediately after she has finished pouring, one of her friends drinks 100 mL from his glass and Lizzie refills it.

How much juice is left in the jug?

A  850 mL

B  900 mL

C  950 mL

D  1000 mL

E  1100 mL

## STRATEGY

Read the question and determine what is required. We first need to determine how much juice is in the jug to begin with. We know the mark for 3 L so can easily work out where 2 L and 1 L would be on the jug.

The amount of juice is 2.5 L and that is 2500 mL. Now, six lots of 250 mL are removed. 6 × 250 = 1500. (If each glass holds 250 mL, then two glasses will hold 500 mL. As 3 × 500 is 1500, the six glasses hold 1500 mL.) So, after all the glasses are filled, 1000 mL remains in the jug (2500 – 1500 = 1000). Then another 100 mL is poured out so 900 mL remain in the jug. **The correct answer is B**.

## SAMPLE QUESTION 2

Meg wants to watch a television program that will start at 1910. 'It will start in a quarter of an hour,' she tells her friend after looking at her watch, which uses 12-hour time.

What must be the time on Meg's watch?

| 8:55 | 7:25 | 6:55 | 6:25 | 7:55 |
|------|------|------|------|------|
| A | B | C | D | E |

## STRATEGY

Read the question carefully and take time to think. The time of the television program is given in 24-hour time, so that needs to be changed to 12-hour time. 1910 is 7:10 pm. (1200 is 12 noon. Subtracting 12 from 19 gives the amount of time, in hours, after 12 noon.) Now, 7:10 pm is a quarter of an hour after the time on Meg's watch. A quarter of an hour is 15 minutes so we need to find the time 15 minutes before 7:10 pm. 10 minutes earlier is 7 pm and 5 minutes before that is 6:55. **The correct answer is C**.

# PRACTICE QUESTIONS

**1** Sally's parents leave at 6:30 pm on Friday for a weekend in Melbourne. They are away for 63 hours. When will they arrive home?

A 9:30 am Sunday
B 9:30 pm Monday
C 7:30 am Monday
D 9:30 am Monday
E 7:30 pm Sunday

**2** One side of square B is four times the length of square A. How many times greater is the area of square B than the area of square A?

Not to scale

A 8 times
B 16 times
C 64 times
D 4 times
E 32 times

**3** A recipe uses 125 g of butter. Nathan has this amount on a plate that he has placed on the scale.

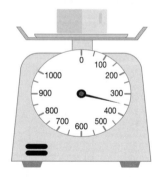

If the plate weighs 210 g, which statement is correct?

A Nathan needs 15 g less butter.
B Nathan needs 15 g more butter.
C Nathan needs 35 g less butter.
D Nathan needs 35 g more butter.
E Nathan has the correct amount.

**4** A landscaper is paving a patio. He must work out the length of the side marked X. What will it be?

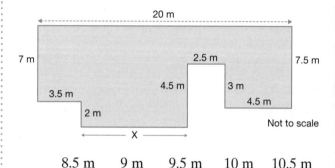

Not to scale

| 8.5 m | 9 m | 9.5 m | 10 m | 10.5 m |
|-------|-----|-------|------|--------|
| A | B | C | D | E |

**5** These two rectangles have the same area.

Not to scale

Which is correct?

A The rectangles have the same perimeter.
B The perimeter of rectangle P is 1 cm less than the perimeter of rectangle Q.
C The perimeter of rectangle P is 2 cm less than the perimeter of rectangle Q.
D The perimeter of rectangle P is 1 cm more than the perimeter of rectangle Q.
E The perimeter of rectangle P is 2 cm more than the perimeter of rectangle Q.

☞ **Answers and explanations on page 112**

# Interpreting graphs and tables

**ACTIVITY:** Often information is displayed in a graph or a table and it is important to be able to understand what is being presented. You should be familiar with the different types of graphs.

## SAMPLE QUESTION 1

In Nicknack Public School, the sportsmistress counted the number of children in the different age groups and came up with the following figures:

| 8 years | 34 |
|---|---|
| 9 years | 60 |
| 10 years | 86 |
| 11 years | 101 |
| 12 years and over | 65 |

The sportsmistress preferred to give the information to the Principal in the form of a graph and she produced the figure below, not bothering about putting the categories (age groups) in any precise order or naming them. But she got one wrong. Which one?

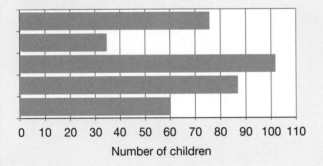

A  8 years

B  9 years

C  10 years

D  11 years

E  12 years and over

## STRATEGY

In this graph, the categories have deliberately not been shown in order to test your reading of graphs. You must transfer the information given to you about the numbers in age groups to the values of the bars on the graph. Only one is wrong so you should be able to identify four of the five age groups. Some are not exactly on a value line so you have to estimate their values.

Starting from the bar at the bottom, it is just on the 60 line (60 children in that age group) and you can write **9 years** beside that bar. The next bar up is between the 80 and 90 line but slightly closer to the 90; look at the figures and you will see the **10 years** group is 86, so you can write that in. The next one up is just over the 100 line, obviously the **11 years** group (101). The next bar (the fourth category up from the bottom) has a value between 30 and 40 but a little closer to 30; look at the list and you see that the **8 years** group has 34 so write it in. The last bar (the top one) appears to be exactly halfway between the 70 and 80 lines, at least in the 74–76 range. No age group has that figure so the wrong one must be **12 years**, the only one not accounted for, giving **answer E**.

## SAMPLE QUESTION 2

Lauren charts the results in her weekly spelling tests for the term on a line graph.

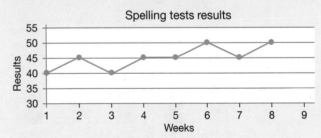

Lauren doesn't have time to record her mark in the ninth week's test. What would it need to have been for her to maintain her average score?

| 44 | 45 | 46 | 47 | 48 |
|---|---|---|---|---|
| A | B | C | D | E |

## STRATEGY

You need to find the average score. Usually, to find the average we add all the scores and divide by the number of scores. Here the scores are graphed and that means there is a much easier way to 'see' the average. The two scores of 50 are balanced by the two scores of 40 and all the other scores are 45, so the average of all the scores must be 45. **The correct answer is B.**

# PRACTICE QUESTIONS

**1** These are the distances jumped by the first six competitors in the 10-year boys' long jump:

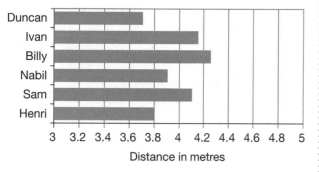

Distance in metres

Which answer is false?

**A** Nabil was fourth.

**B** Sam jumped 4.20 m.

**C** Ivan was second.

**D** Billy won.

**E** Henri jumped 3.8 m.

**2** Here is a column graph of the percentages of sales in a school canteen for one term:

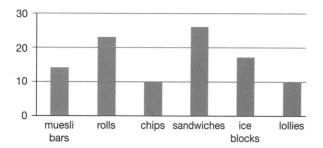

If next term all the children buying lollies changed to buying chips, on the graph

**A** you would need to extend the values by another line.

**B** chips would become second most popular.

**C** ice blocks would be least popular.

**D** chips would become third most popular.

**E** together chips and muesli bars would be about the same as sandwiches.

**3** Lauren charts the results in her weekly maths tests for the term on a line graph.

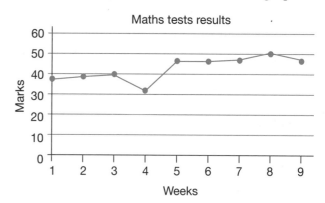

Weeks

Here are three statements about the graph:

1 Every week Lauren improved her maths result.

2 Lauren's biggest weekly improvement was between week 4 and week 5.

3 From week 5 to week 9, Lauren never scored less than 80%.

Which of these statements must be correct?

**A** statement 2 only

**B** statements 1 and 2 only

**C** statements 2 and 3 only

**D** statements 1 and 3 only

**E** statements 1, 2 and 3

☞ **Answers and explanations on page 112**

# SAMPLE TEST

*Read the text below then answer the questions.*

Mrs Darling loved to have everything just so, and Mr Darling had a passion for being exactly like his neighbours; so, of course, they had a nurse. As they were poor, owing to the amount of milk the children drank, this nurse was a prim Newfoundland dog, called Nana, who had belonged to no one in particular until the Darlings engaged her. She had always thought children important, however, and the Darlings had become acquainted with her in Kensington Gardens, where she spent most of her spare time peeping into perambulators, and was much hated by careless nursemaids, whom she followed to their homes and complained of to their mistresses.

She proved to be quite a treasure of a nurse. How thorough she was at bath-time, and up at any moment of the night if one of her charges made the slightest cry. Of course her kennel was in the nursery. She had a genius for knowing when a cough is a thing to have no patience with and when it needs stocking around your throat. She believed to her last day in old-fashioned remedies like rhubarb leaf, and made sounds of contempt over all this new-fangled talk about germs, and so on. It was a lesson in propriety to see her escorting the children to school, walking sedately by their side when they were well behaved, and butting them back into line if they strayed. On John's footer days she never once forgot his sweater, and she usually carried an umbrella in her mouth in case of rain. There is a room in the basement of Miss Fulsom's school where the nurses wait. They sat on forms, while Nana lay on the floor, but that was the only difference. They affected to ignore her as of an inferior social status to themselves, and she despised their light talk. She resented visits to the nursery from Mrs Darling's friends, but if they did come she first whipped off Michael's pinafore and put him into the one with blue braiding, and smoothed out Wendy and made a dash at John's hair.

No nursery could possibly have been conducted more correctly, and Mr Darling knew it, yet he sometimes wondered uneasily whether the neighbours talked.

He had his position in the city to consider.

From *Peter Pan* by JM Barrie

## SAMPLE TEST

For questions **1–5**, choose the option (**A, B, C or D**) which you think best answers the question.

**1**  Mr Darling wants to be _____ his neighbours.

A  just like

B  different from

C  alienated from

D  distinguishable from

**2**  Why was Nana 'hated by careless nursemaids'?

A  She was hated by everyone.

B  They were jealous of her.

C  They were afraid she'd tell on them.

D  She had threatened to bite them.

**3**  Nana's behaviour as a nurse is always

A  well mannered and gentle.

B  prim and proper.

C  resentful and crabby.

D  thoughtful but foolish.

**4**  The Darling family can be described as

A  conventional.

B  normal.

C  typical.

D  highly unusual.

**5**  Which provides the most convincing evidence that this story is pure fantasy?

A  the relationship between Mr and Mrs Darling

B  the fear Nana creates in the other nurses

C  the behaviour of Nana

D  what Mr Darling's business associates would think

☞ **Answers and explanations on pages 113–115**

## SAMPLE TEST

*Read the poem below by Andrew Barton 'Banjo' Paterson then answer the questions.*

### Weary Will

The strongest creature for his size
But least equipped for combat
That dwells beneath Australian skies
Is Weary Will the Wombat.

He digs his homestead underground,
He's neither shrewd nor clever;
For kangaroos can leap and bound
But wombats dig forever.

The boundary rider's netting fence
Excites his irritation;
It is to his untutored sense
His pet abomination.

And when to pass it he desires,
Upon his task he'll centre
And dig a hole beneath the wires
Through which the dingoes enter.

And when to block the hole they strain
With logs and stones and rubble,
Bill Wombat digs it out again
Without the slightest trouble.

The boundary rider bows to fate,
Admits he's made a blunder
And rigs a little swinging gate
To let Bill Wombat under.

So most contentedly he goes
Between his haunt and burrow:
He does the only thing he knows,
And does it very thorough.

From *The Animals Noah Forgot* by AB 'Banjo' Paterson

For questions **6–9**, choose the option (**A, B, C** or **D**) which you think best answers the question.

6. The poet thinks Weary Will is
   A helpful and polite.
   B lazy and contented.
   C deliberately annoying.
   D strong but not very smart.

7. Which adjective best describes the wombat?
   A bored
   B persistent
   C depressed
   D vengeful

8. What does the wombat do that annoys the boundary rider?
   A He keeps getting through the gate.
   B He wears himself out.
   C He digs holes under the fence .
   D He is not very clever.

9. The tone of the poem is mainly
   A serious.
   B lighthearted.
   C irritable.
   D pessimistic.

☞ **Answers and explanations on pages 113–115**

## SAMPLE TEST

*Read the text below then answer the questions*

Five sentences have been removed from the text. Choose from the sentences **(A–F)** the one which fits each gap **(10–14)**. There is one extra sentence which you do not need to use.

### Snubbies

In 2005 snubfin dolphins, affectionately known as snubbies, were recognised as a new species of Australian dolphin. They are different from other species of dolphins in that their dorsal fins tend to be smaller and stubbier. **10** _____ Most dolphins have beaks but this species has rounded melon-shaped beakless heads.

Australian snubfin dolphins inhabit coastal waters from Brisbane in Queensland to Broome in Western Australia. **11** _____ River and creek mouths are favourite habitats. They tend to stay together in small groups usually of about four to six but sometimes larger.

Dolphins sleep differently from humans as they have to remain conscious to control their breathing. **12** _____ They are able to alternate the halves so they can get rest but still remain partly conscious at all times. When sleeping they often lie still on the surface of the water or swim slowly close to the surface often beside another dolphin.

A major threat to their survival over time is their becoming entangled in nets—caught accidentally in fishing nets or trapped in shark-proof nets, for example. **13** _____ This has been caused by increased commercial development of coastal areas and overfishing of their prey. Their reproduction rate is slow. **14** _____ While they are not yet described as endangered, they are considered vulnerable.

| A | They allow one half of their brains to sleep at a time. |
| B | They don't begin to breed until aged about nine and produce only one calf every few years. |
| C | Another major threat is habitat destruction. |
| D | They are also found as far north as Papua New Guinea. |
| E | They communicate with each other using clicks, whistles and squeaks. |
| F | (Dorsal fins in dolphins are like thumb prints in humans—they can be used to identify individuals.) |

☞ **Answers and explanations on pages 113–115**

# SAMPLE TEST

*Read the four texts below on the theme of bird life.*

For questions **15–20**, choose the option (**A, B, C** or **D**) which you think best answers the question.

Which text …

| | | |
|---|---|---|
| points out the importance of caring for the environment? | **15** | _____ |
| is a spoken text? | **16** | _____ |
| describes a bird with excellent sight? | **17** | _____ |
| uses a technical term that means someone who studies birds? | **18** | _____ |
| describes the most extraordinary achievement? | **19** | _____ |
| explains how technology helped a bird? | **20** | _____ |

---

**TEXT A**

Dear Uncle Bill

As you are an ornithologist, I thought you'd be interested to hear about our research project this term. In groups of three we had to find three statements from the internet about a bird native to Australia. Then we had to find ways to check its accuracy. My group chose magpies.

The statements we selected were:

1  There are nine species of magpies indicated by different feather patterns. (Suki)

2  Magpies are excellent mimics. (Mary Lyn)

3  Magpies are unable to recognise human faces. (Geoff)

I worked on the first statement. I took photos of the magpies in our garden each day for a month. I emailed several of my friends who live interstate and asked them to take photos of the magpies in their areas. When I compared their photos with mine, I found three distinctly different black-and-white feather patterns. While this didn't prove the statement was correct, it did confirm that the feather patterns of magpies differ in different areas.

While I was observing the magpies each day I noticed some were imitating kookaburras. Before doing this project, I doubt if I'd have noticed!

Love

Suki

---

☞ **Answers and explanations on pages 113–115**

## SAMPLE TEST

**TEXT B**

### The Eagle

He clasps the crag with crooked hands;
Close to the sun in lonely lands,
Ring'd with the azure world, he stands.

The wrinkled sea beneath him crawls;
He watches from his mountain walls,
And like a thunderbolt he falls.

By Alfred, Lord Tennyson

**TEXT C**

And to end our bulletin we bring you rather special news about a duck whose life has suddenly taken a turn for the better—thanks to our local primary school.

It all began when Daisy Duck lost her foot. Mr and Mrs Fluff, her owners, think it was bitten off by their tortoise who is known to get rather snappy at times. Mr Right, their next-door neighbour, fears he may unintentionally have run over Daisy's foot with his tractor. And the Fluff's dog looks guilty every time Daisy wobbles past.

The villagers are well aware that laying blame as to who is the culprit will not get Daisy a new foot. The vet has done her best. She's given her antibiotics to take and she's bound up her leg. But the life of a duck who has to wobble and bumble around is a difficult one.

Enter the caring children of our local primary school. With the help of their teachers, a group of concerned students made Daisy a new foot. They used their new 3D printer to fashion a foot that could be fitted onto her leg. Mr Avian, a spokesperson for the school, said the children have plans to make Daisy a second foot that she can wear when swimming. Well done, Leeland Primary.

**TEXT D**

*Circle* by Jeannie Baker is a book I love reading over and over. It is about birds called Bar-tailed Godwits. They are famous for flying a very long way without stopping. They fly from Alaska in the arctic north to Australia and New Zealand in the south. Then after feeding and resting they fly back again, making a circle of flight.

Each illustration is a collage. The colours are beautiful and I keep wanting to touch things in the pictures such as the knitted blanket on the bed, the wavy grass where the fox hunts and the soft fluffy chicks.

Another reason I love this book is because it shows you what happens in the real world—the circle of life. You see how the way we treat our own environment affects the lives of other living things. It makes you care about the world.

# SAMPLE TEST

**1** There were five competitors in the high jump at the school sports carnival. Jenny won the competition. Tabatha finished in front of Myra but behind Katie. Cheryn did better than Katie. In what position did Tabatha finish?

A 2nd    B 3rd    C 4th    D 5th

**2** A tree in Mr Smith's street was dying because someone had poisoned it. A police officer told Mr Smith that whoever had poisoned the tree must have wanted the tree to die because it blocked their view of the harbour. This person must also have had the opportunity to poison the tree.

Based on the above information, which one of the following must be true?

A If Mr Smith did not poison the tree, he must not have had the opportunity.

B If Mr Smith did not poison the tree, it cannot have been blocking his view.

C If the tree was not blocking Mr Smith's view of the harbour, he cannot have poisoned the tree.

D If the tree blocked Mr Smith's view of the harbour and he also had the opportunity, he must have poisoned the tree.

**3** What is the next number in this series?

     4   12   9   27   24   72   ?

A 75     B 69     C 16     D 81

**4** To be a successful mountain climber you need to overcome both physical and mental obstacles. You need to have endurance and persistence so that you keep going even when your body is exhausted. You also need to be able to think strategically and assess risks so you know when you should descend.

**Lola:** 'Mimi led the cross-country team to success last term. She planned their whole strategy. She also runs marathons whenever she can. She'd be a successful mountain climber for sure.'

**Conner:** 'Finn is really persistent. He would not give up until he made the cross-country team even though he is not that good at running. But I don't think he likes heights. So mountain climbing is definitely not for him.'

If the information in the box is true, whose reasoning is correct?

A Lola only

B Conner only

C Both Lola and Conner

D Neither Lola nor Conner

**5** Which shape is the mirror image of Figure 1 if the mirror is placed vertically as shown?

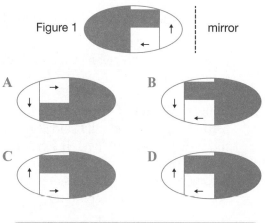

☞ **Answers and explanations on pages 115–117**

## SAMPLE TEST

**6** At what time on a 24-hour digital clock will the digits showing add up to the greatest total?

A 7:59 pm    B 11:59 pm

C 9:59 pm    D 9:59 am

**7**
> Every morning, summer and winter, Na gets up in the cold for a dawn swim at the local beach.

**Ria:** 'You love the cold!'

**Na:** 'No, I hate the cold!'

**Ria:** 'Why do you go swimming when it's so cold then?'

**Na:** 'It's the only time I have. And I soon get warm.'

Which assumption has Ria made in order to draw her conclusion?

A Na loves the cold.

B Na is too busy to swim at any other time.

C Everyone who swims when it's cold loves the cold.

D Everyone who swims when it's cold loves to swim.

**8** When Anita told Olly she was thinking of getting a pet snake, Olly said: 'Snakes shouldn't be kept as pets. It's cruel to keep them in captivity. Snakes don't belong inside cramped glass tanks. They belong in their natural habitat.'

Which one of these statements, if true, most **strengthens** Olly's argument?

A Snakes in captivity need to be fed rabbits, rats, mice and other small animals.

B Snakes in captivity cannot engage in natural behaviours like burrowing, climbing trees or travelling long distances.

C Many people are frightened of snakes.

D Snakes don't generally like being held.

**9** Looking from this direction, how many cubes are entirely out of sight?

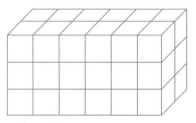

A 8    B 12    C 10    D 18

**10** If Yusaf does not eat breakfast, then he will likely be hungry by the time he gets to the oval.

If he is hungry, then he will not play well at the baseball tryouts.

If he plays well at the baseball tryouts, then he might be offered a place on the team. Otherwise there is no way he will get offered a place.

If the above statements are correct, which one of the following is **not** possible?

A Yusaf did not eat breakfast but was offered a place on the team.

B Yusaf ate breakfast but did not get offered a place on the team.

C Yusaf was hungry at the tryouts but was offered a place on the team.

D Yusaf played well at the tryouts but did not get offered a place on the team.

☞ **Answers and explanations on pages 115–117**

## SAMPLE TEST

**11** A dance troupe is appearing in town this month. The first show is on Friday 13 and the final one is on Sunday 29. There will be a show every night of the week plus afternoon shows every Saturday.

How many shows will there be altogether?

A 19   B 20   C 21   D 22

**12** Five people—Alice, Dane, Georgie, Kahlia and Martin—have garages at the base of an apartment building. The garages are all in a row and are numbered from 1 to 5.

| 1 | 2 | 3 | 4 | 5 |
|---|---|---|---|---|
|   |   |   |   |   |

Dane's garage is a lower number than Martin's.

Alice's garage number is higher than Georgie's and less than Dane's.

Kahlia's garage is somewhere between that of Georgie and of Alice.

Who has garage number 3?

A Alice          B Dane
C Georgie        D Kahlia

**13** When the local council suggested they would close the sculpture park, Arlo's mother wrote a letter to the editor of the newspaper.

Arlo's mother wrote: 'If the sculpture park closes it will hurt the economy. So we must keep it open.'

Which assumption has Arlo's mother made in order to draw her conclusion?

A The sculpture park should not be closed.

B We should not do something that will hurt the economy.

C If the sculpture park closes it will hurt the economy.

D Arlo's mother likes visiting the sculpture park.

**14** The voting age should be lowered to 16. Young people today are more mature than young people were in the past. They deserve to have a say on decisions that will affect their future and the future of the world they live in. Their voices need to be heard. And voting is the best way to be heard.

Which one of these statements, if true, most **weakens** the above argument?

A Young people have studied Citizenship at school.

B Having the right to vote would get young people interested in politics.

C Research shows many 16 year olds are well informed and want to make changes.

D Research shows the brains of 16 year olds are not fully mature.

**15** Six people travelled to a conference. Blake and Kelly arrived at the same time. Finn arrived an hour before Blake. Alice arrived half an hour before Finn and half an hour after Natalie. Amina arrived $2\frac{1}{2}$ hours after Natalie. Kelly arrived at 9:30 am.

Which of these is **not** true?

A Alice arrived at 8:00 am.

B Natalie arrived first.

C Amina arrived $1\frac{1}{2}$ hours after Finn.

D Kelly arrived $1\frac{1}{2}$ hours after Natalie.

**16** A survey was done of pet owners. There were 49 cat owners included in the survey and altogether they had a total of 72 cats. Some of the owners had two cats but none of them had more than two.

How many of the cat owners had exactly one cat?

A 23      B 24      C 25      D 26

☞ **Answers and explanations on pages 115–117**

## SAMPLE TEST

 **17**

There are two ways to qualify to enter the annual State Junior Art Contest: by creating at least three major artworks during the year or by winning a previous art contest during the year. This year, ten students from Ying's school have qualified to enter the Art Contest.

**Ying:** 'I know a total of six artworks by students at our school have won contests during the year. So that means more than half our qualifiers must be contest winners.'

Which one of the following sentences shows the mistake Ying has made?

A Some students may have created more than three major artworks during the year.

B The number of artworks made during the year may be higher than in other years.

C Some of the students may have won more than one art contest during the year.

D Some students who won art contests in the past may also have created three major artworks during the year.

 **18** Five dogs ran an agility course with 10 obstacles.
- Nugget was slower than Rosie but Rosie was slower than Fish.
- Truffles cleared all the obstacles but took the longest.
- Rosie finished second but missed two obstacles.
- Maisie cleared more obstacles than Rosie but finished after her.
- Fish was faster than Maisie but missed three obstacles.

 Which one of these sentences **cannot** be true?

A Maisie cleared fewer obstacles than Truffles.

B Fish was faster than Nugget.

C Fish was not the first to finish the course.

D Fish cleared the least number of obstacles.

**19** A group of people at a party are playing a game. Vincent, Ruby, Cooper and Paige each make two statements. The statements of one of the four are both true. All other statements are false. The other people in the group have to decide who is telling the truth.

Ruby says: 'I am the oldest. Vincent is the youngest.'

Vincent says: 'I am the oldest. Cooper is the youngest.'

Paige says: 'I am the youngest. Vincent is older than Cooper.'

Cooper says: 'I am the youngest. Paige is older than Ruby.'

Who is telling the truth?

A Ruby      B Vincent

C Paige      D Cooper

 **20** Reading a book is healthier than watching television. Reading exercises your brain. Rather than passively taking in information watching television, reading requires your full attention. It exercises your imagination, vocabulary and other brain functions.

Which of these statements, if true, most **strengthens** the above argument?

A Watching television reduces the ability to focus and recall information.

B Some television shows and movies are based on books.

C Reading a book is slower than watching a television show.

D Reading increases language and reasoning skills.

☞ **Answers and explanations on pages 115–117**

# SAMPLE TEST

**1** Jack is making a set of steps. He needs 6 cubes when the steps are 3 high. How many more cubes will he need if the steps are 6 high?

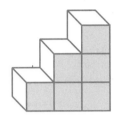

**A** 15 cubes

**B** 18 cubes

**C** 6 cubes

**D** 12 cubes

**E** 9 cubes

**2** If 140 marbles are placed equally into 15 bags, each bag has 9 marbles and there are 5 left over.

Which of these number sentences shows that information?

**A** $9 + 15 \times 5 = 140$

**B** $9 \times 15 + 5 = 140$

**C** $9 \times 15 - 5 = 140$

**D** $5 \times 15 + 9 = 140$

**E** $5 \times 15 - 9 = 140$

**3** A rectangle has a perimeter of 44 cm. A smaller rectangle is cut from the larger one as shown.

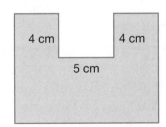

What is the perimeter of the shaded shape?

**A** 26 cm  **B** 36 cm  **C** 52 cm

**D** 57 cm  **E** 62 cm

**4** Mick rolls a normal dice and gets a 3. Then Mary rolls the same dice.

What is the probability that Mary rolls a larger number than Mick?

| $\frac{1}{2}$ | $\frac{1}{3}$ | $\frac{2}{5}$ | $\frac{3}{5}$ | $\frac{1}{6}$ |
|---|---|---|---|---|
| **A** | **B** | **C** | **D** | **E** |

**5** Bernie has a ruler that is broken. The ruler measures in centimetres, but only some of the numbers can be seen. Bernie wants to measure the length of his pencil and finds that it is equal to the length of two of his toy cars.

If the two cars are the same length, how long is the pencil?

**A** 11 cm

**B** 12 cm

**C** 13 cm

**D** 14 cm

**E** 15 cm

**6** A prism has a pentagonal base. What is the sum of the number of faces, the number of edges and the number of vertices?

| 22 | 26 | 28 | 30 | 32 |
|---|---|---|---|---|
| **A** | **B** | **C** | **D** | **E** |

**7** The sign below appears on a map. Which direction is north-east?

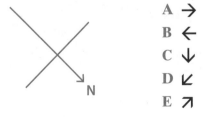

**A** →

**B** ←

**C** ↓

**D** ↙

**E** ↗

☞ **Answers and explanations on pages 117–118**

## SAMPLE TEST

**8** Nadine wants to know how much her dog weighs. She stands on her scales twice, once holding the dog and once without. This is what the scales show.

How much does the dog weigh?

**A** 6 kg      **B** 8 kg      **C** 13 kg
**D** 16 kg    **E** 18 kg

**9** 3 □ 3 ÷ 3 + 3 △ 3 = 4

Two operation signs could replace □ and △ to make this number sentence true. Which of these shows a correct pair of signs?

X  □ = + and △ = −
Y  □ = + and △ = ÷
Z  □ = × and △ = ÷

**A** X only
**B** Y only
**C** Z only
**D** X and Z only
**E** X, Y or Z

**10** A feature wall is made from blocks of the same size. $\frac{2}{5}$ of all the blocks will be white. The rest will be black, apart from the grey blocks shown in the diagram.

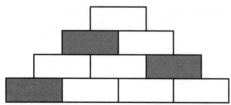

How many blocks will be black?

| 1 | 2 | 3 | 4 | 5 |
|---|---|---|---|---|
| A | B | C | D | E |

**11** Elaine started with an odd number less than 10. She multiplied it by 5, added 3, divided that answer by 2 and then subtracted 1. Her answer was 8.

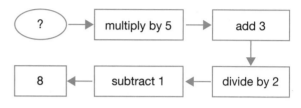

What number did Elaine begin with?

| 1 | 3 | 5 | 7 | 9 |
|---|---|---|---|---|
| A | B | C | D | E |

**12** Below is an ad for a skiing holiday.

If Joe took the 7-day offer and had skiing lessons each day and Betty took the 5-day offer and also had skiing lessons each day, how much more would Joe's holiday cost than Betty's?

| $299 | $284 | $269 | $259 | $239 |
|------|------|------|------|------|
| A | B | C | D | E |

☞ **Answers and explanations on pages 117–118**

## SAMPLE TEST

**13** A train was due to arrive at 1425 but was three-quarters of an hour late. When did it arrive, in 12-hour time?

A  5 am

B  5 pm

C  3 pm

D  5:10 pm

E  3:10 pm

**14** The graph refers to the ages, in January, of students in a Year 5 class.

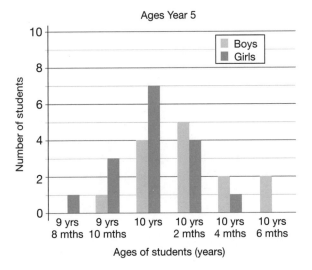

One of the students made these statements.

1. There are more girls than boys in the class.

2. At 10 years of age the girls are taller than the boys.

3. The girls tend to be older on average than the boys.

From the information in the graph, which statements are correct?

A  none of them

B  1 only

C  3 only

D  1 and 3 only

E  all of them

**15** Which of these nets could be folded to form a triangular pyramid?

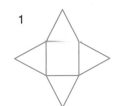
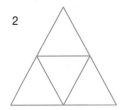
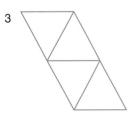

A  1 only

B  2 only

C  3 only

D  2 and 3 only

E  1, 2 and 3

**16** What is the next number in this sequence?

2  4  3  6  5  10  9  18  17  ?

| 16 | 36 | 24 | 26 | 34 |
|----|----|----|----|----|
| A | B | C | D | E |

**17** How many lines of symmetry does this figure have?

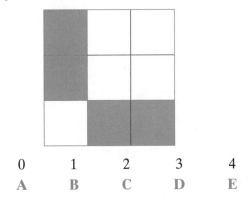

| 0 | 1 | 2 | 3 | 4 |
|---|---|---|---|---|
| A | B | C | D | E |

☞ **Answers and explanations on pages 117–118**

## SAMPLE TEST

**18** Five friends—Carrie, John, Angus, Robbie and Thanh—were collecting stamps. All collected a different number of stamps. Thanh collected the most, 25, and John the least, 19. Angus collected two more than Robbie but one fewer than Carrie.

Which must be true?

A  Angus collected 22 stamps.
B  Robbie collected 23 stamps.
C  Thanh collected one more than Carrie.
D  Robbie collected two more than John.
E  Carrie collected three more than Robbie.

**19** There are 24 cans of tomatoes packed tightly in each case. The top of each can has a radius of 5 cm.

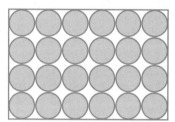

What will be the area, in centimetres squared, of the top of the case?

|  200  |  240  |  600  |  2400  |  6000  |
|:---:|:---:|:---:|:---:|:---:|
|  A  |  B  |  C  |  D  |  E  |

**20** In this magic square the total of each row, each column and each diagonal is the same. What number should be where X is?

| 30 |   | 28 |
|:---:|:---:|:---:|
| 29 |   |   |
| X |   | 32 |

|  27  |  31  |  33  |  34  |  35  |
|:---:|:---:|:---:|:---:|:---:|
|  A  |  B  |  C  |  D  |  E  |

☞ **Answers and explanations on pages 117–118**

# Identifying the meaning of a phrase in context

**ACTIVITY:** You have to work out the context that gives meaning to the phrase. The context is everything that influences, acts upon or is connected with the word in the text.

*Read the text below then answer the question.*

> 'Marilla, can I go over to see Diana just for a minute?' asked Anne, running breathlessly down from the east gable one February evening.
>
> 'I don't see what you want to be traipsing about after dark for,' said Marilla shortly. 'You and Diana walked home from school together and then stood down there in the snow for half an hour more, your tongues going the whole blessed time, clickety-clack. So I don't think you're very badly off to see her again.'
>
> 'But she wants to see me,' pleaded Anne. 'She has something very important to tell me.'
>
> 'How do you know she has?'
>
> 'Because she just signalled to me from her window … Diana has just signalled five flashes, and I'm really suffering to know what it is.'
>
> 'Well, you needn't suffer any longer,' said Marilla sarcastically. 'You can go, but you're to be back here in just ten minutes, remember that.'
>
> From *Anne of Green Gables* by LM Montgomery

## SAMPLE QUESTION

What do the words 'traipsing about' mean?

A  walking quietly

B  walking about needlessly

C  jogging energetically

D  leapfrogging

## STRATEGY

Words can change their meanings in different contexts so it is essential to think about the context: where the phrase occurs in the text and how it fits into the whole of the text.

Traipsing about usually means moving without an end in sight. The context for the phrase 'traipsing about' in this text is that it is said by Marilla who disapproves of Anne going to see Diana in the dark, particularly when she's just seen her earlier that day. You can work out that the phrase expresses Marilla's feelings that her journey is unnecessary and a waste of time.

Now look at options **A–D** and decide which best answers the question.

**B is correct**. The word 'needlessly' suggests Anne's journey has no real purpose; she'll just be walking about unnecessarily. This picks up on Marilla's disapproval of the idea.

**A is incorrect**. This is not usually part of the meaning of the phrase and there is no evidence to suggest Marilla thinks Anne will walk 'quietly'. Furthermore Marilla's disapproval is not conveyed by these words.

**C is incorrect**. The word 'traipsing' does not suggest fast, purposeful movement.

**D is incorrect**. Leapfrogging is not an action that makes sense in this context.

# Making a judgement about a character and their relationship with another character

**ACTIVITY:** You need to look at what each character says and does, and work out how the situation they are in affects how they act towards each other.

*Read the text below then answer the question.*

'Marilla, can I go over to see Diana just for a minute?' asked Anne, running breathlessly down from the east gable one February evening.

'I don't see what you want to be traipsing about after dark for,' said Marilla shortly. 'You and Diana walked home from school together and then stood down there in the snow for half an hour more, your tongues going the whole blessed time, clickety-clack. So I don't think you're very badly off to see her again.'

'But she wants to see me,' pleaded Anne. 'She has something very important to tell me.'

'How do you know she has?'

'Because she just signalled to me from her window … Diana has just signalled five flashes, and I'm really suffering to know what it is.'

'Well, you needn't suffer any longer,' said Marilla sarcastically. 'You can go, but you're to be back here in just ten minutes, remember that.'

From *Anne of Green Gables* by LM Montgomery

## SAMPLE QUESTION

How would you describe Anne's personality?

A cool and calm

B ill-willed and stubborn

C passionate and intense

D cheeky and warm-hearted

## STRATEGY

You need to judge how the author presents the character (in this case, Anne) by looking at what she says and does, and how others act towards her.

Anne's actions and reactions are intense: she runs 'breathlessly' to ask her question of Marilla, then pleads with her and follows this up with a passionate request claiming she is 'suffering' to know Diana's secret. Marilla's sarcastic response suggests she is used to Anne's exaggerations and takes them in her stride. Marilla's critical attitude is shown to be understandable but at the same time there is sympathy for how deeply Anne feels things. It is made clear that Anne is close to Diana and values her friendship.

Now look at options **A–D** and decide which best answers the question.

**C is correct**. Anne is loyal and passionate about her friendship with Diana and reveals a depth of feeling that is intense when she pleads her cause to Marilla.

**A is incorrect**. There is nothing cool or calm about Anne's behaviour.

**B is incorrect**. Although Anne pleads her case strongly and doesn't want to give up her visit, she shows no sign of ill will.

**D is incorrect**. Despite evidence that Anne is warm-hearted in the way she feels about her friendship with Diana, she is not at all cheeky when begging Marilla to let her go to Diana's house.

# PRACTICE QUESTIONS

*Read the text below then answer the questions.*

'Marilla, can I go over to see Diana just for a minute?' asked Anne, running breathlessly down from the east gable one February evening.

'I don't see what you want to be traipsing about after dark for,' said Marilla shortly. 'You and Diana walked home from school together and then stood down there in the snow for half an hour more, your tongues going the whole blessed time, clickety-clack. So I don't think you're very badly off to see her again.'

'But she wants to see me,' pleaded Anne. 'She has something very important to tell me.'

'How do you know she has?'

'Because she just signalled to me from her window … Diana has just signalled five flashes, and I'm really suffering to know what it is.'

'Well, you needn't suffer any longer,' said Marilla sarcastically. 'You can go, but you're to be back here in just ten minutes, remember that.'

From *Anne of Green Gables* by LM Montgomery

---

**1** What do the words 'the whole blessed time' mean in the text?

A every single irritating moment

B every precious moment

C all day long

D without stopping

---

**2** How would you describe Marilla's response to Anne's request?

A unkind

B unfair

C reasonable

D loving

☞ **Answers and explanations on page 119**

# Interpreting meanings by working out what is implied

**ACTIVITY:** You have to look for meanings that aren't directly stated in the text. These meanings will be suggested or hinted at by the tone used or from clues that alert you to what is implied.

*Read the poem below by Robert Frost then answer the question.*

> ### A Time to Talk
> When a friend calls to me from the road
> And slows his horse to a meaning walk,
> I don't stand still and look around
> On all the hills I haven't hoed,
> And shout from where I am, What is it?
> No, not as there is a time to talk.
> I thrust my hoe in the mellow ground,
> Blade-end up and five feet tall,
> And plod: I go up to the stone wall
> For a friendly visit.

## SAMPLE QUESTION

Why doesn't the narrator shout 'What is it?'
A  He thinks his friend won't hear him.
B  He wants a break from hoeing.
C  He can never resist a chat with anyone.
D  He values their friendship.

## STRATEGY

You need to think about the values of the person who decides not to say these words (in this case, the narrator speaking in the first person) and the situation he is in.

The narrator shares his thoughts in a way that sounds trustworthy and believable. He believes there is a time to talk—a time when it matters to show your friend respect by making an effort to talk to them properly. He leaves his hoe and goes to his friend, turning the occasion into a friendly visit. Friendship is clearly something he values.

Now look at options **A–D** and decide which best answers the question.

**D is correct**. When the narrator thinks about why he stops working and goes to where his friend is for a talk, he is enabling a friendly visit between them. He values friendship highly and likes to honour it by this simple gesture.

**A is incorrect**. If he can hear his friend's call to him, then his friend could hear his reply. He doesn't want to just call to his friend; he thinks his friend deserves a proper conversation.

**B is incorrect**. The speaker might want a break from hoeing but this isn't his reason for stopping work and going to talk to his friend.

**C is incorrect**. There is no evidence to suggest the narrator can't resist a chat.

# Identifying the tone of the poem as a whole

**ACTIVITY:** You need to work out how features of the poem such as voice, language and rhythm create the tone and mood of the poem as a whole.

*Read the poem below by Robert Frost then answer the question.*

> ## A Time to Talk
> When a friend calls to me from the road
> And slows his horse to a meaning walk,
> I don't stand still and look around
> On all the hills I haven't hoed,
> And shout from where I am, What is it?
> No, not as there is a time to talk.
> I thrust my hoe in the mellow ground,
> Blade-end up and five feet tall,
> And plod: I go up to the stone wall
> For a friendly visit.

## SAMPLE QUESTION

How would you describe the tone of the poem?
A  reflective and conversational
B  witty and argumentative
C  anxious and concerned
D  sad and worried

## STRATEGY

You can identify the tone by thinking about the poet's attitude to the subject of the poem. In some writing the poet has a different attitude from the narrator, which will affect the poem's meaning, although this is not the case with this poem. Looking at the language and rhythms of the voice that narrates the poem can help you make a judgement about its tone.

As you read the poem, it is as if you are listening to someone thinking aloud using ordinary, everyday language. The lines flow gracefully into one another, forming two thought units. The narrator thinks about why he didn't keep working and then why he stopped. The last line is very simple in its expression but it is the essence of why he behaved as he did: his actions led to a 'friendly visit', something of great importance to him.

Now look at options **A–D** and decide which best answers the question.

**A is correct**. The tone of the poem is reflective as the narrator thinks over his actions and their motivation. His thoughts are reported as though he is having a conversation with himself.

**B is incorrect**. The poem is neither witty nor amusing, and although it is as though a conversation is going on, he is not arguing with himself; rather he is just reflecting.

**C and D are incorrect**. The speaking voice is confident and assured about what is important to him. The narrator shows no signs of anxiety, concern or worry and is glad rather than sad.

## PRACTICE QUESTIONS

*Read the extract from the poem below by Robert Frost then answer the questions.*

### Birches

When I see birches bend to left and right
Across the lines of straighter darker trees,
I like to think some boy's been swinging them.
But swinging doesn't bend them down to stay.
Ice-storms do that. Often you must have seen them
Loaded with ice a sunny winter morning
After a rain. They click upon themselves
As the breeze rises, and turn many-coloured
As the stir cracks and crazes their enamel.
Soon the sun's warmth makes them shed crystal shells
Shattering and avalanching on the snow-crust—
Such heaps of broken glass to sweep away
You'd think the inner dome of heaven had fallen.

1   The words 'Ice-storms do that' imply that the birches
    A   are bent by their power.
    B   look magical when it snows.
    C   have very flexible boughs.
    D   are difficult to ride during ice-storms.

2   The poet's attitude towards the idea of a boy swinging on the birches is
    A   disapproving.
    B   approving.
    C   critical.
    D   anxious.

☞ **Answers and explanations on page 119**

# Identifying how information and ideas are sequenced

**ACTIVITY:** Sequencing involves putting ideas and information in a logical order. To work out how sentences are connected to each other within a text you need to consider what goes before and after, and how it fits into the whole text.

**SAMPLE QUESTIONS**

*Read the text below then answer the questions.*

Three sentences have been removed from the text. Choose from the sentences (**A–D**) the one which fits each gap (**1–3**). There is one extra sentence which you do not need to use.

---

## Lightning Ridge

Lightning Ridge in NSW has a misleading name. **1** _____ It is actually a low line of hills on a plain that stretches to the western horizon.

The name originated when a shepherd, his dog and 600 sheep were killed by lightning.
**2** _____ A plaque recalling the incident is at the turn-off to the town.

Lightning Ridge is famous for opals. They were discovered here in 1873. Since then the area has produced some of the world's finest opals. **3** _____ The quality of the Ridge opals is superior, however, with the most valuable being the black opals.

---

| A | The district does not produce as many opals as Coober Pedy, SA. |
|---|---|
| B | This is because 'Ridge' is an exaggeration. |
| C | On rare occasions opalised fossils have been found from the dinosaur age. |
| D | They had been sheltering in nearby scrub. |

## Identifying how information and ideas are sequenced

### STRATEGY

Read the whole text first so you know what it is about. Then read the missing sentences and find the first space, numbered 1. Think about the subject of its paragraph. Look closely at the sentences before and after the space then work out the sequence of ideas and information. Repeat this procedure for questions 2 and 3.

You need to select the sentence from **A–D** that best connects with these sentences.

1   **B is correct.** In paragraph one the author comments on the name Lightning Ridge, a place in NSW. The sentence before the space says the name is misleading. The missing sentence explains why: This is because 'Ridge' is an exaggeration. The sentence that follows explains its physical features are low hills on a plain, implying this is less elevated than a ridge.

2   **D is correct.** Paragraph two is about how Lightning Ridge got its name. The sentence before the space explains the incident in which lightning struck a shepherd and his sheep, an event which provides the origin of the name. This sentence gives more information about where they were when lightning struck: They had been sheltering in nearby scrub. The sentence that follows notes there is a plaque commemorating this incident.

3   **A is correct.** Paragraph three is about the opals found at Lightning Ridge. The sentence before the space notes Lightning Ridge has produced some of the world's best opals. This sentence acknowledges, however, that it produces fewer opals than Coober Pedy: The district does not produce as many opals as Coober Pedy, SA. The sentence following implies that while Lightning Ridge may produce fewer opals, their quality is superior to those from Coober Pedy.

The unused sentence is C.

*Read the text below then answer the questions.*

Three sentences have been removed from the text. Choose from the sentences (**A–D**) the one which fits each gap (**1–3**). There is one extra sentence which you do not need to use.

### Quicksand

Quicksand occurs in many places across Australia. **1** _____ This could be on the beach at low tide, or where creeks and rivers flow into the sea.

Fine granular material (such as sand, silt or clay) gets mixed with water and if the water in the sand cannot get away, then a liquefied soil or quicksand is formed. **2** _____ When you step on the quicksand, the water is forced out and your limbs are caught in the vice-like grip of the remaining sand.

Human beings can't drown in quicksand. **3** _____ They are unlikely to sink lower than about waist high level. However, if you were to be trapped in quicksand on a beach when the tide was coming in, you could well drown.

| | |
|---|---|
| **A** | You usually find it where water and loose soil meet. |
| **B** | In the 60s and 70s, quicksand often featured in the plots of movies. |
| **C** | Humans are not as dense as quicksand. |
| **D** | This type of soil is unable to support weight. |

☞ Answers and explanations on page 119

# Comparing aspects of texts such as forms, structures, ideas and language use

**ACTIVITY:** You have to understand what each text is about, its form and how it is written. This will enable you to compare the texts so you can choose the one that best provides an answer to the question.

## SAMPLE QUESTIONS

*Read the two texts below on the theme of mutiny.*

For questions **1–3**, choose the option (**A** or **B**) which you think best answers the question.

Which text …

contains a lively argument?   **1** _____

includes a character who describes his own bravery?   **2** _____

ends on a note of tension?   **3** _____

---

### TEXT A

Tuesday 28, 1789. Just before sun-rising, while I [William Bligh] was yet asleep, Mr. Christian [Fletcher], with the master at arms, gunner's mate, and Thomas Burkitt, seaman, came into my cabin, and seizing me tied my hands with a cord behind my back, threatening me with instant death if I spoke or made the least noise: I however called as loud as I could in hopes of assistance; but they had already secured the officers who were not of their party by placing sentinels at their doors … Particular people were called on to go into the boat and were hurried over the side; whence I concluded that with these people I was to be set adrift …

From *A Voyage to the South Sea* by William Bligh

---

### TEXT B

'To cast us adrift here in an open boat is to consign us to destruction. Think of my wife and family!'

'No, Captain Bligh,' replied Christian, sternly; 'if you had any honour things had not come to this; and if you had any regard for your wife and family, you should have thought of them before and not behaved so much like a villain. It is too late. You have treated me like a dog all the voyage. Come, sir, your officers and men are now in the boat, and you must go with them. If you attempt resistance you shall be put to death.'

[…]

As regards Bligh, it is sufficient to say that he performed one of the most remarkable boat-voyages on record.

[…]

But we leave him now to trace those incidents which result from the display of his other qualities — ungovernable passion, overbearing impetuosity, and incomprehensible meanness.

From *The Lonely Island* by RM Ballantyne

---

## Comparing aspects of texts such as forms, structures, ideas and language use

### STRATEGY

When finding which text offers the answer to a question you need to have a good grasp of what each text is about and how it is written. For example, you'll notice Text A is a diary entry written in the first person. The writer is reporting a mutiny which involves his capture by Mr Christian, who threatens his life. Bligh's response is to stand up to the threats as best he can. Text B begins with an angry conversation between the writer of the diary, Captain Bligh, and his captor Christian. The author then offers an analysis of Bligh's character and achievements.

Now look at the questions and decide which text best answers each one.

1   **B is correct.** Text B contains a lively exchange of different opinions between Bligh and Fletcher. Text A is in the first person and does not include dialogue.

2   **A is correct.** Text A includes Bligh's claim that when he was threatened with 'instant death' if he made any noise, he called out as loudly as he could for assistance. Christian, in Text B, may have acted bravely but there is no account of it here.

3   **A is correct.** Text A ends with Bligh concluding he is about to be set adrift in a boat where his life is likely to be in danger. This is a tense, unresolved ending. Text B concludes with the author planning to discuss Bligh's darker side. This arouses interest rather than tension.

# PRACTICE QUESTIONS

*Read the two texts below on the theme of mutiny.*

For questions **1–3**, choose the option (**A** or **B**) which you think best answers the question.

Which text …

refers to an extraordinary achievement?

**1** _____

presents opposing points of view?

**2** _____

suggests Bligh was outnumbered in defeat?

**3** _____

---

**TEXT A**

Tuesday 28, 1789. Just before sun-rising, while I [William Bligh] was yet asleep, Mr. Christian [Fletcher], with the master at arms, gunner's mate, and Thomas Burkitt, seaman, came into my cabin, and seizing me tied my hands with a cord behind my back, threatening me with instant death if I spoke or made the least noise: I however called as loud as I could in hopes of assistance; but they had already secured the officers who were not of their party by placing sentinels at their doors … Particular people were called on to go into the boat and were hurried over the side; whence I concluded that with these people I was to be set adrift …

From *A Voyage to the South Sea* by William Bligh

---

**TEXT B**

'To cast us adrift here in an open boat is to consign us to destruction. Think of my wife and family!'

'No, Captain Bligh,' replied Christian, sternly; 'if you had any honour things had not come to this; and if you had any regard for your wife and family, you should have thought of them before and not behaved so much like a villain. It is too late. You have treated me like a dog all the voyage. Come, sir, your officers and men are now in the boat, and you must go with them. If you attempt resistance you shall be put to death.'

[…]

As regards Bligh, it is sufficient to say that he performed one of the most remarkable boat-voyages on record.

[…]

But we leave him now to trace those incidents which result from the display of his other qualities— ungovernable passion, overbearing impetuosity, and incomprehensible meanness.

From *The Lonely Island* by RM Ballantyne

---

☞ **Answers and explanations on page 120**

# Drawing a conclusion

**ACTIVITY:** You need to evaluate the evidence presented in an argument. A correct conclusion must be supported by evidence. A conclusion is not possible or cannot be true if the evidence does not support it.

## SAMPLE QUESTION 1

In a survey, parents of Year 6 students were asked to identify issues of concern regarding their children. Of most concern were:

- children feeling overwhelmed
- children spending too much time on devices such as laptops and smart phones
- children developing poor sleep habits
- children being bullied.

The survey results showed that parents who were worried about their children feeling overwhelmed were also worried about their children not sleeping. It also showed that everyone who was worried about their child not sleeping was also worried about their child spending too much time on devices but no-one who was worried about their child developing poor sleep habits was also worried about bullying.

The parents of Conrad, Rose, Eric and Carla took part in the survey.

Based on the above information, which one of the following statements **must** be true?

A If Conrad's parents were worried about him spending too much time on devices, they were also worried about him developing poor sleep habits.

B If Rose's parents were not worried about bullying, they were also not worried about her spending too much time on devices.

C If Eric's parents were not worried about Eric feeling overwhelmed, they were also not worried about him developing poor sleep habits.

D If Carla's parents were worried about her feeling overwhelmed, they were not worried about bullying.

### STRATEGY

1 Read the information in the box.
2 Read the question.
3 To answer this question you need to identify whether a conclusion must be true that is not stated in the information provided but instead can be drawn from the information.
4 Read each statement in turn and evaluate if it must be true.

**D is correct.** From the information given, any parent who was worried about their child feeling overwhelmed was also worried about them developing poor sleeping habits and if they were worried about poor sleeping habits, they were not worried about bullying. So statement D must be true.

**A is incorrect.** All the parents who were worried about sleep were worried about time spent on devices. However, the information does not state that all the parents who were worried about time spent on devices were also worried about their child developing poor sleep habits.

**B is incorrect.** The text does not state that parents who weren't worried about bullying also weren't worried about time spent on devices.

**C is incorrect.** Just because the information says that everyone who was worried their child was feeling overwhelmed was also worried about their child developing poor sleep habits, it does not automatically mean that if parents are not worried about their child being overwhelmed then they are not worried about their child's sleep habits.

## *Drawing a conclusion*

**SAMPLE QUESTION 2**

The Council is going to change its on-street, car-parking laws for streets adjacent to The Willows retail area and restaurant precinct. The change will allow people who live locally to park from 5 pm to 8 am as long as they obtain a parking sticker from the Council to display on their windscreens. All visitors to the area and residents parking outside the 5 pm to 8 am time slot will only be able to park for two hours. Previously, people visiting or working in The Willows were taking up all the street parking spaces so residents had nowhere to park for the night.

If the above information is true, only one of the sentences below **cannot** be true. Which one?

A **Alicia:** 'I live next to The Willows so when I get home from work at 6 pm I will be able to park till I leave for work at 8 am.'

B **Lata:** 'I live about twenty minutes drive from The Willows but I like to go to restaurants there so now if I get there at 6 pm, I'll have to finish dinner and remove my car by 8 pm.'

C **Phil:** 'The new laws are inconvenient because if I want to take two hours to shop or dine, I won't be able to bring my car.'

D **Douglas:** 'I live near The Willows and go grocery shopping there early in the afternoon so now I have to do it within two hours.'

**STRATEGY**

1  Read the information in the box.

2  Read the question.

3  To answer this question you need to identify a conclusion that cannot be true based on the information provided.

4  Read each statement in turn and evaluate if it cannot be true.

C is correct. This conclusion cannot be true. Phil has concluded incorrectly that he won't be able to park close by for two hours. However, the information clearly states that visitors to the area and residents parking outside the 5 pm to 8 am time slot will be able to park for two hours.

**A is incorrect**. The information tells you that people who live locally can park from 5 pm to 8 am as long as they obtain a parking sticker from Council to display on their windscreens. So Alicia is correct in concluding that as a resident of The Willows she will be able to park from 6 pm until she leaves for work at 8 am.

**B is incorrect**. The information tells you that people can park for two hours to go to restaurants in The Willows. Therefore Lata is correct when she concludes that if she gets there at 6 pm, she'll have to finish dinner and remove her car by 8 pm.

**D is incorrect**. Douglas correctly concludes that when he drives to The Willows for grocery shopping in the afternoon, he will have to complete his shopping within two hours.

# Identifying an assumption

**ACTIVITY:** You need to evaluate the evidence and the conclusion drawn from that evidence to work out any assumptions made in reaching this conclusion. Note that it is easy to make assumptions that lead to incorrect conclusions.

**SAMPLE QUESTION 1**

**Jennifer:** 'When the alarm went off everyone came onto the street, out of nearby buildings, to see what was happening. They stood around watching and waiting, wondering what was going on. It seems the jewellery store had been burgled. A window had been smashed so the burglar could gain entry. I saw one man running down the street away from the area just after the store's alarm went off.'

**Ishaan:** "He must have been the burglar making his getaway.'

Which of the following sentences is the assumption Ishaan has made to draw his conclusion?

A  Anyone in the vicinity of a burglary must be a suspect in that burglary.

B  Anyone running away from a store after its alarm goes off must be a burglar.

C  The man running away from the jewellery store was a burglar.

D  Everyone runs when they hear an alarm.

## STRATEGY

1  Read the information.

2  Read the question.

3  Firstly identify Ishaan's conclusion and the evidence he used to draw his conclusion. Ishaan's conclusion is that a man seen running down the street was the burglar. The evidence Ishaan uses is that the man was seen running away from the area after the alarm went off, while everyone else in the vicinity seems to have been standing around on the street.

4  Evaluate each answer option in light of Ishaan's conclusion and the evidence.

**B is correct.** Ishaan's assumption must be that anyone running away from a store after an alarm goes off must be a burglar.

**A is incorrect.** For this to have been Ishaan's assumption, all the spectators on the street would have been suspects and this was not Ishaan's conclusion.

**C is incorrect.** This is a restatement of Ishaan's conclusion.

**D is incorrect.** This statement contradicts evidence in the text that people stood around in the street after the alarm went off. Not everyone ran.

## Identifying an assumption

**SAMPLE QUESTION 2**

The new housing development means that large areas of the eucalypt forest have been cut down. Developers were required to leave corridors of trees in place so that the native koala population would be able to move along these corridors between more forested areas. The koalas walk along the ground from tree to tree. While on the ground, koalas are in danger from pets—particularly dogs. Once the housing development is completed and the homes occupied, the annual number of koalas hurt or killed by dogs will be higher than before construction began.

Which of the following is an assumption made by the writer of the above text?

A  The number of koalas hit by trucks will not increase when the development is completed.

B  The number of koalas killed or hurt by dogs during the past ten years has been very low.

C  The koala hospital will require extra funding to support the welfare of koalas attacked by dogs.

D  People occupying the new homes will have dogs and those dogs will attack koalas.

**STRATEGY**

1  Read the information.

2  Read the question.

3  Firstly identify the argument and its conclusion. The writer concludes that once the homes are occupied, the annual number of koalas hurt or killed by dogs will be higher than before construction began.

4  Evaluate each answer option in light of the writer's conclusion and the evidence.

**D is correct.** To draw their conclusion the writer must have assumed people occupying the new homes will have dogs and those dogs will be allowed to roam freely in the forest and wildlife corridor to attack koalas.

**A is incorrect.** The statement that the number of koalas hit by trucks will not increase when the development is completed is likely to be true because you would assume the trucks will no longer be required. However, this assumption is irrelevant to the argument about dogs and does not lead to the conclusion drawn by the writer.

**B is incorrect.** The statement that the number of koalas killed or hurt by dogs has been very low during the past ten years is irrelevant because in this situation past performance is no indicator of future performance once the development is competed and occupiers with pets move into the new housing. This assumption does not lead to the conclusion drawn by the writer.

**C is incorrect.** The statement that the koala hospital will require extra funding to support the welfare of koalas attacked by dogs might be true but is irrelevant to the argument. This assumption does not lead to the conclusion drawn by the arguer.

# Assessing the impact of additional evidence

**ACTIVITY:** You need to evaluate a claim or argument and judge whether additional evidence will weaken or strengthen that argument.

**SAMPLE QUESTION 1**

**Umi:** 'I must be good at multitasking because I have so much work to juggle and I manage to get it done.'

**Andrew:** 'You aren't really multitasking. You are doing a number of tasks in quick succession and probably not focusing on doing any of them to your full ability. Very few people can multitask effectively. I think you'd be better off focusing on one task at a time. That would be less stressful too.'

Which one of these statements, if true, most **strengthens** Andrew's argument?

A  Constantly switching between tasks means you are more likely to make mistakes.

B  The more complex the tasks, the harder it becomes to multitask effectively.

C  Multitasking divides your attention between tasks.

D  Multitasking affects some people's ability to focus for any length of time.

## STRATEGY

1  Read the texts.

2  Read the question.

3  Work out what argument Andrew is making in his comments to Umi. Andrew says Umi should focus on one task at a time instead of multitasking because multitasking is difficult to manage effectively and is stressful.

4  Consider the answer options. Any statement about the ineffectiveness of multitasking will strengthen Andrew's argument.

5  Judge which answer is correct. Check all the answer options to ensure you have chosen the correct answer.

**A is correct.** This statement most strengthens Andrew's argument.

**B is incorrect.** This statement strengthens Andrew's argument because it states that more complex tasks make it harder to multitask effectively. However, this statement is not as strong as A which is about making mistakes.

**C is incorrect.** This is a restatement of a comment Andrew has already made.

**D is incorrect.** This statement strengthens Andrew's argument but is not as strong a statement as A. The statement that multitasking affects **some** people's ability to focus is not as strong an argument for Umi as the statement that says she is **more likely** to make mistakes when switching between tasks in an attempt to multitask.

## Assessing the impact of additional evidence

**SAMPLE QUESTION 2**

The use of computers and other digital learning tools in the classroom enhances learning and supports teaching. Computers enable students to work at their own pace so education can be more flexible and targeted towards each individual student's needs.

Which one of these statements, if true, most **weakens** the above argument?

A Social interaction and opportunities to learn through collaboration are reduced when individuals work online.

B Children already spend more time on digital devices than is healthy for their physical wellbeing.

C It's easy to get distracted and distract others by games and internet content when using digital technology.

D Technology can make learning more interesting because of the availability of visual aids.

**STRATEGY**

1 Read the text.

2 Read the question.

3 Identify the argumentIdentify the argument: that digital technology enhances learning.

4 Read and evaluate each statement. Any statement that detracts from, contradicts or undermines the argument that digital technology enhances learning will weaken the argument.

**C is correct**. This statement weakens the argument that digital technology enhances learning.

**A is incorrect**. This statement is about student collaboration being reduced rather than learning being reduced, so it is a side issue and does not specifically weaken the argument that digital technology enhances learning.

**B is incorrect**. This statement might be true but not does not specifically weaken the argument.

**D is incorrect**. This statement strengthens the argument because it provides extra evidence or reason to use digital technology to enhance learning.

# Checking reasoning to detect errors

**ACTIVITY:** You need to analyse the reasoning used in an argument or claim. If the reasoning holds up, the claim might be accepted. If the reasoning does not make sense or is flawed, the claim or argument can be rejected.

## SAMPLE QUESTION 1

> Food scientists and food technologists are those who study, research, innovate and improve food products and processes to ensure safety, quality and nutritional adequacy are maintained in food products for a vast range of consumer needs.
>
> To become a successful food technologist you also need to have good communication skills, strong Science and Maths skills, an ability to work hygienically and to follow regulations, and strong attention to detail.

**Gerri:** 'Lianne loves anything to do with food. She's always experimenting in the kitchen and creating her own fabulous recipes. She'll become an excellent food technologist.'

**Heath:** 'Zac is very studious and pays attention to detail. He can follow rules and comply with regulations. He is a person who works best collaboratively and socially but, as he has excellent communication skills, I know he'd be happy in a laboratory conducting research and being a successful food technologist.'

If the information in the box is true, whose reasoning is correct?

**A** Gerri only      **B** Heath only      **C** Both Gerri and Heath      **D** Neither Gerri nor Heath

### STRATEGY

1  Read the information in the box and then the statements made by Gerri and Heath.

2  Read the question.

3  Evaluate the statements made by Gerri and Heath. Compare their statements about the abilities of Zac and Lianne with the criteria required to become a successful food technologist.

4  When you work out whether Gerri or Heath (or both) are correct, use a process of elimination to select your answer option.

**D is correct.** Neither Gerri nor Heath uses correct reasoning.

**A is incorrect.** Gerri uses incorrect reasoning. Lianne's only skill is creating her own recipes.

Gerri cannot reasonably assert that Lianne will become an excellent food technologist when evaluating the skills required of a successful food technologist.

**B is incorrect.** Heath is incorrect because, while Zac has the general skills required to become a successful food technologist (he is studious, pays attention to detail, can follow rules and comply with regulations, and has excellent communication skills), Heath acknowledges that Zac is a person who works best collaboratively and socially. Heath cannot reasonably assert that Zac would be happy in a laboratory conducting research and being a successful food technologist.

**C is incorrect.** Both Gerri and Heath use incorrect reasoning.

## Checking reasoning to detect errors

**SAMPLE QUESTION 2**

The art competition awards prizes for first, second and third. The prizes are awarded at the discretion of the judging panel. A prize is also awarded to the artwork voted most popular by members of the public.

**Kirsten:** 'I know that four art works will be awarded a prize. I hope my sculpture is one of the four lucky winners.'

Which one of the following sentences shows the mistake Kirsten has made?

A  Some artists might deserve a prize but not receive one.

B  The artwork most popular with the public might also receive a prize from the judging panel.

C  Not many members of the public bother to vote or have seen the exhibition.

D  The judges have not been advised about which artwork won the public vote.

**STRATEGY**

1  Read the information in the box and then the statement made by Kirsten.

2  Read the question.

3  Evaluate Kirsten's statement in light of the information in the box.

4  Judge which answer option shows Kirsten's mistake.

**B is correct.** To calculate the number of prizes available, Kirsten has added the three prizes awarded by the judging panel to the prize for the public vote to mistakenly assert that four artworks will be awarded a prize. However, the artwork that was most popular with the public could also be awarded a place prize by the judges so that one artist could receive two prizes. This would mean only three artworks would be awarded a prize.

**The other options are incorrect.** These statements might be true but they aren't mistakes made by Kirsten.

# PRACTICE QUESTIONS

1   'Whoever put the inflatable Santa Claus on the roof overnight must have had both an opportunity and a motive.'

If this is true, which one of these sentences must also be true?

A   If Scarlet had both an opportunity and a motive, she must have put the inflatable Santa Claus on the roof overnight.

B   If Scarlet did not have a motive she can't have climbed onto the roof.

C   If Scarlet didn't put the inflatable Santa Claus on the roof overnight, she must not have had an opportunity.

D   If Scarlet didn't put the inflatable Santa Claus on the roof overnight, she must not have had a motive.

2   Jarrod joined the crowd watching the fire burn down the house at the end of the street. He hadn't called the fire brigade but wondered what was taking the fire engine so long to arrive.

Which assumption did Jarrod make to draw his conclusion?

A   that someone had called the fire brigade

B   that the fire engine must be caught in a traffic jam

C   that firefighters were not needed at the site

D   that an arsonist had set fire to the house

3   Lauren told Jeremy she intended to give up gymnastics so she could focus on her dance career. Jeremy argued, 'You don't need to give up gymnastics just because you want a career as a dancer. You've always enjoyed gymnastics and it helps to keep you fit for dancing.'

Which one of these statements, if true, most **strengthens** Jeremy's argument?

A   Gymnasts can practise skills such as handsprings, cartwheels and vaulting.

B   Lauren's dance teacher thinks Lauren needs to develop more flexibility.

C   Dancing helps keep you fit for gymnastics.

D   Gymnastics and dancing both require balance and coordination.

4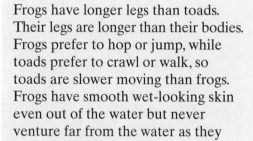

Frogs have longer legs than toads. Their legs are longer than their bodies. Frogs prefer to hop or jump, while toads prefer to crawl or walk, so toads are slower moving than frogs. Frogs have smooth wet-looking skin even out of the water but never venture far from the water as they lose moisture very easily. Toads have dry warty-looking skin.

If the information in the box is true, whose reasoning is correct?

A   **Viggo:** 'Look! There's a frog walking through the grass. I know it's a frog because it's walking, not hopping or jumping, but it's a long way from its pond.'

B   **Gillian:** 'I think that's a toad walking through the grass. A frog would not venture so far from the water. And look at its skin. It's smooth.'

C   **Travis:** 'Its skin is not smooth and shiny. And it's got short legs. I think it could be a toad.'

D   **Haruna:** 'I'm sure it's a frog looking for a pond. Its skin is not that warty looking.'

☞ **Answers and explanations on pages 120–121**

# Spatial reasoning

**ACTIVITY:** The skills needed in spatial reasoning have many elements. Students must be able to visualise both 2D and 3D shapes and objects and manipulate them in their mind. They must have an understanding of symmetry, transformations, nets and properties of regular shapes.

## SAMPLE QUESTION 1

Wally is using a pattern of tiles as a feature in his bathroom. So far he has completed six columns with two tiles in each column.

Wally wants the pattern to be symmetrical with one vertical line of symmetry lying along a join between tiles. How many more columns of two tiles could Wally add to complete the pattern?

A 6 only

B 2 or 6

C 4 or 6

D 2, 5 or 6

## STRATEGY

It is important to read the question carefully and make sure you understand what you are required to find. Here the pattern is to be continued with more columns of two tiles. The result needs to be symmetrical with a vertical ( I ) line of symmetry. So you need to imagine the pattern folded so that the two halves match exactly. This can happen if either 4 columns or 6 columns are added. **The correct answer is C.**

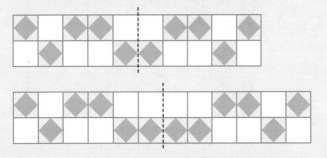

## SAMPLE QUESTION 2

A cube has a grey face, a white face and faces with a diagonal cross, a circle, a diamond and a straight cross. These are the six faces of the cube.

Here are two different views of the cube:

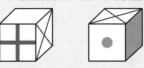

Ezra made these statements:

X  The white face must be opposite the face with the circle.

Y  The grey face must be opposite the face with the straight cross.

Which statements are correct?

A  X only          B  Y only

C  Both X and Y    D  Neither X nor Y

## STRATEGY

Here you need to determine which, if either, of the statements X and Y are correct. You need to look at the two views of the cube and determine where all the faces lie. Five of the faces can be seen. One face, the diagonal cross, can be seen in both views. We can see that it is next to four of the faces. The face that cannot be seen is the diamond so it must be opposite the diagonal cross. In the first view the face with the circle and the grey face must be on the bottom and back in some order. Considering that order we can see (in our mind's eye) that the grey face must be on the back and the circle on the bottom. So the white face must be opposite the face with the circle and the grey face must be opposite the face with the straight cross. Both statements X and Y are correct. **The correct answer is C.**

## PRACTICE QUESTIONS

**1** Cheralyn looks at a sign on a waiting room wall and sees:

Looking up, she sees the sign in the mirror on the opposite wall. How does the sign look in the mirror?

A

B

C

D

**2** A floor is being tiled using two similar tiles in different orientations. One tile is missing.

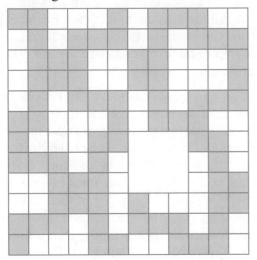

How should the missing tile appear?

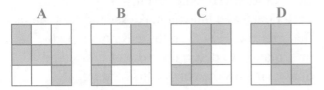

**3** Charlotte has some blocks, each made up of five hexagons. She is using the blocks to form a triangle. The blocks can be rotated or reflected. Charlotte needs three more blocks to cover the white spaces and complete the triangle.

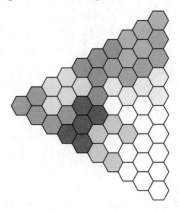

Which of these will she not use?

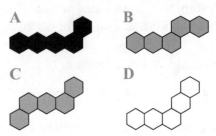

**4** Which of these shapes have been joined together, with no overlap, to make the shaded figure? They may have been used a number of times and may be turned round.

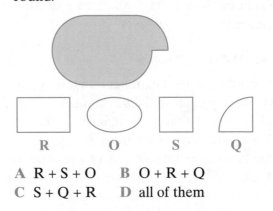

A  R + S + O      B  O + R + Q
C  S + Q + R      D  all of them

☞ **Answers and explanations on page 121**

# Logical reasoning

**ACTIVITY:** The requirement for this type of reasoning is the ability to think clearly, use common sense and identify the key elements of the question. Often it is possible to find contradictions in the given information which allow you to determine what must be true and what must be false.

## SAMPLE QUESTION 1

Five witnesses to an incident involving a dog were asked what breed it was. Lee said it was a boxer, Tom said it was a Doberman and Amy said it wasn't a bulldog. Erica said the dog wasn't a Doberman and Henry said it wasn't a Dalmatian. Except for one person, they were all correct.

What type of dog was it?

A  boxer                          B  Doberman
C  bulldog                        D  Dalmatian

### STRATEGY

The approach for questions like this one involves looking for contradictions in the given statements. It is important to read the question carefully and take note of all information. Here we know that exactly one of the five witnesses made a statement that was not correct.

Tom and Erica gave contradictory statements. The dog can't be both a Doberman and not a Doberman, so either Tom or Erica is the witness who was not correct. This means Lee, Amy and Henry must all have been correct. As Lee's statement is correct, the dog must have been a boxer. **The correct answer is A.**

The person who was incorrect was Tom. The dog was not a Doberman, not a bulldog and not a Dalmatian. It was a boxer.

## SAMPLE QUESTION 2

A waiter at a restaurant became totally confused when three sisters talked to him about celebrating the birthday of one of them. Erin, Grace and Shayna each made two statements. The statements from one sister were both true, the statements from another sister were both false and the other sister made one true statement and one false statement.

Erin said:      'It is my birthday. I am older than Grace.'
Grace said:    'It is my birthday. I am the oldest and Erin is older than Shayna.'
Shayna said:  'It is my birthday. Grace is older than Erin.'

Which of the following **must** be true?
A  It is Erin's birthday.
B  It is Grace's birthday.
C  It is Shayna's birthday.
D  Grace is older than Erin.

### STRATEGY

The first step is to read the question carefully and make sure you understand what is happening. Here there are three sisters who each make two statements but not all of the statements are correct. All the girls claim it is their birthday but only one can be correct. The sister who makes the two true statements must be the one celebrating her birthday.

The false statement of whoever makes one true and one false statement must be 'It is my birthday'. Her second statement must be true. So the second statement of two sisters must be true. Now, consider the second statements of Erin and Shayna. They are contradictions. One must be true and one must be false. As only one of the second statements is false, this means Grace's second statement must be true. So she is the oldest and must therefore be older than Erin. **The correct answer is D.**

Both of Erin's statements must be false and both Grace and Shayna make second statements that are true. However, there is not enough information to determine who of Grace and Shayna makes the correct first statement. Therefore A must be false but we cannot say B or C **must** be true.

# PRACTICE QUESTIONS

**1** Four runners finished a race very closely together and no-one was sure who had won. The runners made the following statements but only one of those statements was correct.

Travis said: 'I didn't win.'

Mitch said: 'Harry won.'

Harry said: 'Ethan won.'

Ethan said: 'Harry is wrong. I didn't win.'

Who won the race?

A Travis

B Mitch

C Harry

D Ethan

**2** A game at a party involves four marbles: one purple, one blue, one red and one green. Four children are each given a marble and have to make two statements about the colour they have and that of one of the others but none of the statements can be true. The other children at the party have to try to work out the correct colour of the marble each child has. The statements were:

**Brittany:** 'Daniel has purple. I have green.'

**Nathan:** 'I have red. Chloe has purple.'

**Daniel:** 'I have green. Brittany has either purple or blue.'

**Chloe:** 'Nathan has blue. I have red.'

Which colour is Chloe's marble?

A purple

B blue

C red

D green

**3** Four people made these statements to the police.

**Ruth:** 'Donald is lying.'

**Keith:** 'Ruth is lying.'

**Isabella:** 'Keith isn't lying.'

**Donald:** 'Both Isabella and Ruth are lying.'

Only one of them was telling the truth. Who was it?

A Ruth

B Keith

C Isabella

D Donald

**4** A cricketer made a statement giving two pieces of information to each of three different friends after a twenty20 match. At least one of the two pieces of information was true.

■ He told Ken he took no wickets but scored 36 runs.

■ He told Joe he did not score 56 runs, he scored 86 runs.

■ He told Luke he took two wickets and scored 36 runs.

Which must be true?

A He scored 36 runs.

B He scored 86 runs.

C He took no wickets.

D He took two wickets.

☞ **Answers and explanations on page 121**

# Solving problems

**ACTIVITY:** Some questions might be quite unusual or different to what has been seen before. It is important to read the question carefully and understand what is required. Take time to think!

Common successful methods of solving problems include making a table; making an organised list; looking for a pattern; using trial and error; drawing a picture or graph; working backwards; solving a similar but simpler problem; and finding a pattern or formula.

Whichever method you choose (and the type of problem often suggests which is best), it is important to remember the time you have to do the test is limited so you cannot afford to follow steps you might otherwise use. For example, there is no need to waste time estimating what the answer might be if the options suggest that anyway.

## SAMPLE QUESTION 1

Five friends—Freya, Henry, Julia, Rory and Stephanie—are fans of five different football teams: the Foxes, Hawks, Jets, Rockets and Stars. No-one is a fan of the team that begins with the same initial as their name. In addition, Henry is not a fan of the Jets, Freya doesn't like the Hawks or the Jets and Stephanie is not a fan of the Foxes, Jets or Hawks.

Of what team is Julia a fan?

A Foxes     B Hawks    C Rockets   D Stars

### STRATEGY

Read the question carefully and make sure you understand what is required. The answer is not immediately obvious so work through the given information and determine what you can.

Stephanie is not a fan of the Foxes, Jets or Hawks nor of the Stars because that team begins with her initial. So Stephanie is a fan of the Rockets.

Freya is not a fan of the Hawks, Jets, Foxes (beginning with her initial) or Rockets (because that is Stephanie). So Freya is a fan of the Stars.

Henry is not a fan of the Jets, Rockets or Stars and he cannot be a fan of the Hawks. So Henry is the Foxes fan.

Therefore Julia cannot be a fan of the Rockets, Stars, Foxes or Jets. So Julia is a fan of the Hawks. **The correct answer is B.**

## SAMPLE QUESTION 2

Bennie is considering buying some books: a novel, a biography and a reference book. Together the novel and the biography cost $38, the novel and the reference book cost $41, and the biography and the reference book cost $45.

What will the three books cost altogether?

A $62        B $80        C $83        D $86

### STRATEGY

Read the question carefully and take time to think. We know the price of all the different combinations of two of the books. So adding the prices will give the cost of two of all the books.

Now, $38 + $41 + $45 = $124. Half of $124 is $62. So the cost of all three books together will be $62. **The correct answer is A.**

It is possible to find the price of the individual books but this is a time-consuming process and is unnecessary. The novel is $17, the biography is $21 and the reference book is $24.

# PRACTICE QUESTIONS

**1** A particular college has students studying four subjects: chemistry, biology, physics and geology. It is known that:

- chemistry is compulsory for anyone studying biology
- some students are studying both physics and geology
- all students studying physics are also studying chemistry
- no students are studying both geology and biology
- fewer students study geology only than study chemistry only.

Which of the four subjects has the most students?

A biology
B chemistry
C geology
D physics

**2** Max has some red, blue, yellow and green marbles in a bag. There are four times as many red marbles as yellow ones and twice as many blue ones as yellow. If he takes a marble from the bag without looking, the probability that it is red or yellow is the same as the probability that it is blue or green.

What is the probability that the marble is green?

A 0.1    B 0.2    C 0.3    D 0.4

**3** Mitchell, Jack and Nathan are three brothers. Mitchell is three times the age of Nathan, who was born 12 years after Mitchell. The sum of all their ages is six times the age of Nathan.

How old is Jack?

A 9    B 10    C 11    D 12

**4** Six children competed in a competition. There were five rounds where points were awarded from 1 to 6 (one child getting 1, 1 getting 2, and so on). After the competition finished the position of each child was recorded, with position 1 being for the child with the most total points. No two children ended up with the same total. The table of results is shown below but round 5 points were left out. Maeve knows she got just 1 point in round 5 and Atticus got the most points in that round.

| Name | Round | | | | | Position |
|------|---|---|---|---|---|---|
| | 1 | 2 | 3 | 4 | 5 | |
| Atticus | 6 | 4 | 1 | 3 | | 1 |
| Chloe | 4 | 1 | 5 | 2 | | 5 |
| Elias | 1 | 5 | 2 | 6 | | 4 |
| Kane | 2 | 6 | 4 | 5 | | 2 |
| Maeve | 5 | 2 | 3 | 4 | | 6 |
| Oscar | 3 | 3 | 6 | 1 | | 3 |

How many points did Oscar get in round 5?

A 2    B 3    C 4    D 5

**5** Georgia used a code to write some simple words. Her words were LION, MUST, PLOD and SAVE.

The code she used was to replace each letter with the number representing its position in the alphabet. For example, HELP would be 851216.

| A | B | C | D | E | F | G | H | I | J | K | L | M |
|---|---|---|---|---|---|---|---|---|---|---|---|---|
| 1 | 2 | 3 | 4 | 5 | 6 | 7 | 8 | 9 | 10 | 11 | 12 | 13 |
| N | O | P | Q | R | S | T | U | V | W | X | Y | Z |
| 14 | 15 | 16 | 17 | 18 | 19 | 20 | 21 | 22 | 23 | 24 | 25 | 26 |

Later Georgia changed her numbers back into words but one of her new words was different to the original word.

For which of her words did Georgia find a different word?

A LION    B MUST    C PLOD    D SAVE

☞ **Answers and explanations on page 122**

# Numerical reasoning

**ACTIVITY:** Many questions require the use of simple numerical rules and processes. They might involve simple arithmetic or fractions, decimals and percentages. Questions test students' understanding of these processes but in general do not require complicated manipulation. It is more a case of using common sense and applying basic mathematical knowledge.

## SAMPLE QUESTION 1

Paula had 100 cows. She sold some to Ed and then sold half of what she had left to Col. Col then sold to Sebastian half of the cows that he had bought from Paula. If Sebastian bought 12 cows from Col, how many did Paula sell to Ed?

| 12 | 24 | 26 | 48 | 52 |
|----|----|----|----|----|
| A  | B  | C  | D  | E  |

### STRATEGY

Read the question carefully and make sure you understand what is required. Here we are looking for the number of cows that Paula first sold. We can work backwards to find the answer.

Sebastian bought 12 cows from Col and that was half of the cows Col had bought from Paula. So Col bought 24 cows from Paula. This was half of what Paula had left after selling some to Ed. So Paula must have had 48 left after selling some to Ed. As Paula began with 100 cows, she must have sold 100 – 48 or 52 to Ed.

We can check the answer by working forwards.

**The correct answer is E.**

## SAMPLE QUESTION 2

Four children take part in a quiz each week. They each receive a score from 1 to 6. These are their results for the first three weeks.

| Name   | Week 1 | Week 2 | Week 3 |
|--------|--------|--------|--------|
| Ivan   | 5      | 6      | 4      |
| Max    | 4      | 3      | 3      |
| Bella  | 2      | 5      | 6      |
| Esther | 3      | 4      | 5      |

After the fourth week all the children had the same total score for the first 4 weeks.

How many points did Esther get in the fourth test?

| 2 | 3 | 4 | 5 | 6 |
|---|---|---|---|---|
| A | B | C | D | E |

### STRATEGY

Read the question carefully and look for the important information. Here they all had the same score after 4 weeks.

After 3 weeks, Ivan has a total score of 15, Max's total is 10, Bella has 13 points and Esther has 12.

Now each week they receive a score from 1 to 6. Ivan must score at least 1 point so his total after 4 weeks must be at least 16.

To have a score of 16 after 4 weeks, Max will need to score 6 points in the fourth test. This is the most that he can score so 16 must be the total that all the children have.

Esther will need to score 4 in the fourth test to increase her total score from 12 to 16.

| Name   | Week 1 | Week 2 | Week 3 | Week 4 | Total |
|--------|--------|--------|--------|--------|-------|
| Ivan   | 5      | 6      | 4      | 1      | 16    |
| Max    | 4      | 3      | 3      | 6      | 16    |
| Bella  | 2      | 5      | 6      | 3      | 16    |
| Esther | 3      | 4      | 5      | 4      | 16    |

**The correct answer is C.**

# PRACTICE QUESTIONS

**1** An 800-seat cinema complex is divided into three theatres. There are 270 seats in Theatre 1 and there are 150 more seats in Theatre 2 than there are in Theatre 3. How many seats are there in Theatre 2?

A 380

B 330

C 415

D 340

E 420

**2** Nan cut five oranges into quarters for her five grandchildren. Susan ate 2 quarters, Mark ate 5 quarters, Jesse ate 3 quarters, Jordan ate 6 quarters and Daniel ate the rest.

How much more orange did Daniel eat than Susan?

| $\frac{1}{4}$ | $\frac{1}{2}$ | $\frac{3}{4}$ | 1 whole | $1\frac{1}{2}$ |
|---|---|---|---|---|
| A | B | C | D | E |

**3** An outdoor setting is for sale for a total price of $1650. The setting consists of a lounge, dining table and six chairs. The lounge is half of the price of the table and chairs. The dining table can also be bought separately at a cost of $100 less than the six chairs.

What is the price of the dining table?

A $500

B $550

C $575

D $600

E $650

**4** How many whole numbers between 1 and 100 are multiples of 6 but not multiples of 7?

| 13 | 12 | 15 | 16 | 14 |
|---|---|---|---|---|
| A | B | C | D | E |

**5** Caleb, Ty, David, Lewis, Hailey and Emma all did a test. Their marks, when arranged in order from highest to lowest, were 92, 89, 87, 87, 83 and 80.

- Caleb and Ty got the same mark.
- Ty got a lower mark than Emma.
- Hailey's mark was lower than David's but higher than Lewis's.

Which might not be true?

A Ty got 4 more marks than Hailey.

B Caleb got a lower mark than David.

C Emma scored 92.

D Lewis scored 80.

E Caleb got a higher mark than Lewis.

**6** Brad is at a market and wants to buy six pies. He notices that four different stalls are selling pies and three of them have special offers.

| Stall owner | Normal price per pie | Special offer |
|---|---|---|
| Riley | $5 | Buy 2 get 1 free |
| Samantha | $3 | —— |
| Harrison | $4 | Buy 2 get the third for half price |
| Stephen | $3.80 | Buy 5 get 1 free |

From which stall owner can Brad buy 6 pies for the least amount?

A Riley

B Samantha

C Harrison

D Stephen

E All the prices are the same.

☞ **Answers and explanations on page 123**

# Working with measurements

**ACTIVITY:** Being able to work with all different types of measurements is very important. This includes length, mass and capacity, area and volume, time and speed. It is necessary to understand and be able to use the different units of measurement. You must also be able to apply the knowledge in practical situations.

## SAMPLE QUESTION 1

A course is being conducted at the local community college and all students must complete 40 hours of attendance. Students attend for 3 hours on Mondays and Wednesdays and 2 hours on Fridays. Eloise starts the course on Monday, 4 June. The second Monday in June is a public holiday and the college will be closed that day. What is the earliest date that Eloise could complete the course?

A  6 July

B  7 July

C  8 July

D  9 July

E  10 July

### STRATEGY

Read the question carefully and interpret all the given information. We need to find the earliest date that Eloise could complete 40 hours of attendance at the college.

First find the hours that she can attend each week: 2 × 3 hours + 2 hours = 8 hours. Now, as 8 × 5 = 40, Eloise could complete the course in 5 full weeks. Because Eloise will miss the Monday of the second week, she will need to attend on the Monday of the sixth week to make up the time. Counting forward by sevens gives the dates of all the Mondays in June: 4, 11, 18, 25. There are 30 days in June so the following Monday will be 2 July and Eloise will finish the course on 9 July. **The correct answer is D.**

## SAMPLE QUESTION 2

This is the plan of the upstairs of a house. Carpet is to be laid in all except the tiled areas.

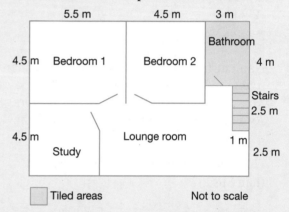

How many square metres (m²) of carpet will be needed?

A  103.5 m²        B  117 m²     C  105 m²

D  102.5 m²        E  112 m²

### STRATEGY

Interpret the question. You need to find the area to be carpeted. The easiest way to do that is to find the total floor area and subtract the area that will be tiled. From the plan we can see the total length is (5.5 + 4.5 + 3) m or 13 m. The width is (4.5 + 4.5) m or 9 m. So the total floor area is (13 × 9) m² or 117 m².

Next step, work out the area not to be carpeted (the tiled sections) in the same way.

Tiled area = Bathroom (3 m × 4m) + Stairs (2.5 m × 1 m).

This becomes Tiled area = 12 m² (Bathroom) + 2.5 m² (Stairs) = 14.5 m².

Finally, subtract: Total area (117 m²) – Tiled area (14.5 m²) = 102.5 m², giving **answer D**.

# PRACTICE QUESTIONS

**1** Yolanda makes tubs of yoghurt in two sizes. The mass of a small tub is 560 g less than the mass of a large tub. The mass of a large tub is five times the mass of a small tub. Yolanda sells the large tubs in boxes of five. What is the mass of a box of large tubs of Yolanda's yoghurt?

| 2.5 kg | 3 kg | 3.5 kg | 4 kg | 4.5 kg |
|--------|------|--------|------|--------|
| **A**  | **B**| **C**  | **D**| **E**  |

The approximate dimensions of a tennis court are shown in the diagram below.

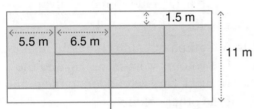

Not to scale

**2** How much larger is the perimeter of the doubles (whole) tennis court than the perimeter of the singles court (the shaded area)?
A  3 m
B  35 m
C  6 m
D  16 m
E  9 m

**3** What is the area of the singles court (the shaded area)?
A  264 m²
B  121 m²
C  228 m²
D  192 m²
E  242 m²

**4** Mr Thrush is an area supervisor living in Grange who, each weekday, travels to a different one of the nearby towns then home again. The distances to each town from Grange are given in the table below:

| Merlot 48 km | Barossa 52 km | Mildara 49 km |
|--------------|---------------|---------------|
| Hunter 95 km | Swan 56 km    |               |

If Mr Thrush's average driving speed on his trips is 80 km/h, how many hours will he spend on the road (driving) during the week?
A  7.5 hours   B  12 hours   C  8 hours
D  10 hours   E  15 hours

**5** If two months before last month had just 28 days, which will be the next month after this month with 31 days with its name containing the letter r?
A  October
B  September
C  November
D  January
E  March

**6** Each edge of a solid cube is 2 cm in length. What will be the mass of the cube if it is made from plastic weighing 1.5 g per cm³?

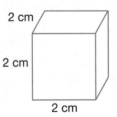

A  6 g
B  8 g
C  9 g
D  12 g
E  15 g

☞ **Answers and explanations on page 123**

# Interpreting graphs and tables

**ACTIVITY:** Often information is presented in a graph or a table. It is important to be able to understand and interpret what is being displayed. You must be aware of the types of problems and issues that can arise. You should be familiar with the different types of graphs and be able to match information given in one form with the same information in a different form.

## SAMPLE QUESTION 1

There were four candidates in an election. The results are shown in the table.

| Candidate | Karl | Petra | Ada | Rhys |
|---|---|---|---|---|
| Number of votes | 25 | 35 | 75 | 45 |

The results were also shown in a pie chart but Karl thinks one of the lines is put in the wrong place.

The line between which two candidates is wrong (if any)?

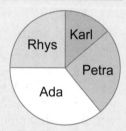

A  Karl and Petra
B  Petra and Ada
C  Ada and Rhys
D  Rhys and Karl
E  None of them

### STRATEGY

From reading the question carefully we know the table is correct but the graph might not be accurate. We need to establish which sectors are correct and in a test situation we will not have a protractor to accurately measure the angles. Begin by looking at the graph. We can immediately see the sectors for Petra and Rhys are the same size, one-quarter of the circle, but from the table we know their numbers of votes are not the same.

The total number of votes is 25 + 35 + 75 + 45 = 180. One-quarter of 180 is 45. So the sector for Rhys is correct but the sector for Petra is not correct. Petra's sector should be smaller and that of either Karl or Ada should be larger. Now, Ada received three times the number of Karl's votes. We can see that Karl's sector is more than one-third the size of Ada's so Karl's sector should not be larger. Ada's sector should be larger.

The line between Petra and Ada is wrong. **The correct answer is B.**

## SAMPLE QUESTION 2

Josh recorded the colour of cars that drove past his house one day. The table shows the results.

| Colour | black | blue | red | silver | white |
|---|---|---|---|---|---|
| Number | 18 | 30 | 24 | 36 | 42 |

Josh drew a graph but, unfortunately, he didn't label it. The colours were mixed up and the number of black cars was added to the number of one of the other colours.

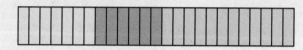

To what colour was the number of black cars added?

A  blue
B  red
C  silver
D  white
E  It is not possible to tell.

### STRATEGY

Read the question carefully and make sure you understand what is required. Here the graph shows four different sections but, from the table, it should be five. The number for black has been combined with one of the others. You need to find which one.

The total colour of cars is 18 + 30 + 24 + 36 + 42 = 150. The graph has been divided into 25 parts. Now, 150 ÷ 25 = 6. So each part represents 6 cars. Dividing each number in the table by 6, we can see there should be 3 parts for black, 5 for blue, 4 for red, 6 for silver and 7 for white. But the graph is divided into 7, 6, 8 and 4 parts.

So the 3 parts for black must have been added to the 5 parts for blue. **The correct answer is A.**

# PRACTICE QUESTIONS

**1** One hundred people were asked which of five fruits were their favourite. The results are shown in this table.

| Type of fruit | Number |
|---|---|
| apple | 16 |
| banana | 28 |
| grapes | 20 |
| orange | 24 |
| peach | 12 |

Alex drew this bar chart to show the results but left out one of the types of fruit.

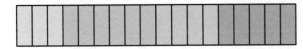

Which fruit was left out?

A apple    B banana    C grapes

D orange    E peach

**2** This column graph charts the costs of the same washing machine at different stores:

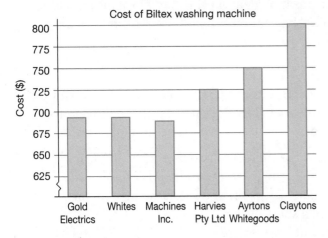

Ayrtons Whitegoods are having a sale with all goods reduced by 10%. Claytons find they have overpriced the Biltex washing machine by $110. Who has the Biltex machine at the cheapest price?

A Machines Inc.    B Gold Electrics

C Ayrtons Whitegoods

D Claytons      E Whites

**3** As part of their Social Science project, 6G collected data on rainfall for the first six months of 1899 and 1900 and drew the following line graph based on the information:

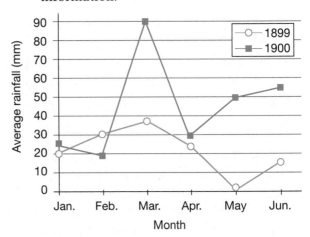

Approximately how much more rain fell in the first six months of 1900 than in 1899?

A 100 mm

B 120 mm

C 140 mm

D 160 mm

E 180 mm

**4** Kai has correctly started to draw a pie chart from the information in the table but the number for Ava is missing.

| Name | Number |
|---|---|
| Pia | 30 |
| Arlo | 10 |
| Max | 25 |
| Finn | 40 |
| Ava | |

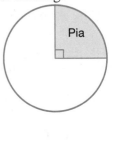

What size angle should Kai use for the sector for Ava?

| 20° | 30° | 45° | 60° | 75° |
|---|---|---|---|---|
| A | B | C | D | E |

☞ **Answers and explanations on page 124**

*Read the text below then answer the questions.*

The day began auspiciously. They had lost no dogs during the night, and they swung out upon the trail and into the silence, the darkness, and the cold with spirits that were fairly light. Bill seemed to have forgotten his forebodings of the previous night, and even waxed facetious with the dogs when, at midday, they overturned the sled on a bad piece of trail.

It was an awkward mix-up. The sled was upside down and jammed between a tree-trunk and a huge rock, and they were forced to unharness the dogs in order to straighten out the tangle. The two men were bent over the sled and trying to right it, when Henry observed One Ear sidling away.

'Here, you, One Ear!' he cried, straightening up and turning around on the dog.

But One Ear broke into a run across the snow, his traces trailing behind him. And there, out in the snow of their back track, was the she-wolf waiting for him. As he neared her, he became suddenly cautious. He slowed down to an alert and mincing walk and then stopped. He regarded her carefully and dubiously, yet desirefully. She seemed to smile at him, showing her teeth in an ingratiating rather than a menacing way. She moved toward him a few steps, playfully, and then halted. One Ear drew near to her, still alert and cautious, his tail and ears in the air, his head held high.

He tried to sniff noses with her, but she retreated playfully and coyly. Every advance on his part was accompanied by a corresponding retreat on her part. Step by step she was luring him away from the security of his human companionship. Once, as though a warning had in vague ways flitted through his intelligence, he turned his head and looked back at the overturned sled, at his team-mates, and at the two men who were calling to him.

[…]

In the meantime, Bill had bethought himself of the rifle. But it was jammed beneath the overturned sled, and by the time Henry had helped him to right the load, One Ear and the she-wolf were too close together and the distance too great to risk a shot.

Too late One Ear learned his mistake. Before they saw the cause, the two men saw him turn and start to run back toward them. Then, approaching at right angles to the trail and cutting off his retreat they saw a dozen wolves, lean and grey, bounding across the snow. On the instant, the she-wolf's coyness and playfulness disappeared. With a snarl she sprang upon One Ear. He thrust her off with his shoulder, and, his retreat cut off and still intent on regaining the sled, he altered his course in an attempt to circle around to it. More wolves were appearing every moment and joining in the chase. The she-wolf was one leap behind One Ear and holding her own.

'Where are you goin'?' Henry suddenly demanded, laying his hand on his partner's arm.

Bill shook it off. 'I won't stand it,' he said. 'They ain't a-goin' to get any more of our dogs if I can help it.'

From *White Fang* by Jack London

## SAMPLE TEST

For questions **1–5**, choose the option (**A, B, C** or **D**) which you think best answers the question.

**1**  What does 'auspiciously' mean?
A regularly
B quickly
C suspiciously
D promisingly

**2**  Why does One Ear sidle away?
A He is attracted by the she-wolf.
B He wants to avoid punishment when the sled overturns.
C He is annoyed with Bill and Henry.
D He wants to get out of helping.

**3**  The she-wolf's purpose in teasing One Ear is to
A please him.
B move him away from Bill and Henry.
C worry him.
D show off her attractiveness.

**4**  What does the she-wolf know that One Ear doesn't?
A that the men want to keep One Ear safe
B that the wolf pack is on its way
C that Bill and Henry will betray One Ear
D that she can run faster than One Ear

**5**  This extract ends on
A a high point of tension.
B a note of pessimism.
C a feeling of despair.
D a sense of triumph.

☞ **Answers and explanations on pages 124–126**

## SAMPLE TEST

*Read the poem below by Sheryl Persson then answer the questions.*

### Visiting the Natural History Museum

Delicate bird entombed in glass
your feathers, flecked with autumn
can never feel the breeze
Perched on silence, snap-fine feet
almost clutch a branch
and your beak is ready to strip a bulrush
Glass eyes accuse me with a fixed stare
as my fingers tap the display case
but it is tuneless      like you
Better to see you ornament a distant sky
better to know you nourish the soil
with your brittle bones
than this

■ For questions **6–9**, choose the option (**A, B, C** or **D**) which you think best answers the question.

**6**   The poet describes the bird as 'entombed' because
  **A** the glass stops the bird from flying away.
  **B** the glass case is also its tomb.
  **C** you can see the bird through the glass.
  **D** the bird can't see through the glass.

**7**   The words 'snap-fine feet' emphasise the bird's
  **A** fragility.
  **B** photogenic qualities.
  **C** sprightliness.
  **D** perfection.

**8**   The poet's visit to the museum evokes her
  **A** irritation.
  **B** appreciation.
  **C** distress.
  **D** delight.

**9**   What is 'this'?
  **A** the death of the bird
  **B** the burial of the bird
  **C** the dead bird being unable to sing
  **D** the dead bird on display, trapped forever

☞ **Answers and explanations on pages 124–126**

## SAMPLE TEST

*Read the text below then answer the questions.*

Five sentences have been removed from the text. Choose from the sentences **(A–F)** the one which fits each gap **(10–14)**. There is one extra sentence which you do not need to use.

---

### The history of spectacles

From far back in human history, people have found ways to improve their sight. It is claimed the Roman Emperor, Nero, watched the gladiator games through two polished emeralds. **10** _____ . There is also evidence the Greeks filled glass bowls with water in order to magnify small print.

Early glasses were soon made with two lenses riveted together. **11** _____ . Various materials such as bone, wood or metal and in later times, wire or leather, were used to house the glass.

In the 1600s the rigid nose bridge appeared and some time after that frames, called temple frames, were made in one piece. **12** _____ . You usually bought these from a pedlar (someone who travels from place to place selling small goods). In the 1800s, rimmed spectacles and monocles came into vogue. The choice of lens was still a matter of trial and error.

It was many years before eye examinations and prescriptions were developed. **13** _____ . This chart is still used today for eyesight tests.

In the early twentieth century, spectacles gained their current form. Styles continue to go in and out of fashion. When sunglasses came into use in the 1930s, this helped change the image of wearing glasses to more of a fashion statement. **14** _____ . In the last few decades, Harry Potter, a character from a successful book and television series, has made wearing glasses very popular, particularly among children.

---

| A | This meant you could wear glasses and leave your hands free. |
|---|---|
| B | They could be held or worn on the face by pinching them tightly onto the nose. |
| C | In 1862 a Dutch ophthalmologist developed an eye chart to measure clarity of vision. |
| D | In the 13th century, Italian monks crafted semi-shaped ground lenses which could be used as magnifying glasses. |
| E | Some people now wear glasses without prescription lenses because they think they make them look attractive. |
| F | No-one is quite sure why this worked for him but it did. |

☞ Answers and explanations on pages 124–126

## SAMPLE TEST

*Read the four texts below on the theme of animal characters.*

For questions **15–20**, choose the option (**A, B, C** or **D**) which you think best answers the question.

Which text …

| | | |
|---|---|---|
| is from an autobiography 'written' by an animal? | **15** | _____ |
| contains a humorous exchange between an animal and a human? | **16** | _____ |
| is about an animal's delight? | **17** | _____ |
| does not include reference to any kind of water? | **18** | _____ |
| includes a kind animal character? | **19** | _____ |
| is about two animal characters? | **20** | _____ |

---

**TEXT A**

He thought his happiness was complete when, as he meandered aimlessly along, suddenly he stood by the edge of a full-fed river. Never in his life had he seen a river before—this sleek, sinuous, full-bodied animal, chasing and chuckling, gripping things with a gurgle and leaving them with a laugh, to fling itself on fresh playmates that shook themselves free, and were caught and held again. All was a-shake and a-shiver—glints and gleams and sparkles, rustle and swirl, chatter and bubble. The Mole was bewitched, entranced, fascinated. By the side of the river he trotted as one trots, when very small, by the side of a man who holds one spellbound by exciting stories; and when tired at last, he sat on the bank, while the river still chattered on to him, a babbling procession of the best stories in the world, sent from the heart of the earth to be told at last to the insatiable sea.

From *The Wind in the Willows* by Kenneth Grahame

---

**TEXT B**

The first place that I can well remember was a large pleasant meadow with a pond of clear water in it. Some shady trees leaned over it, and rushes and water-lilies grew at the deep end. Over the hedge on one side we looked into a plowed field, and on the other we looked over a gate at our master's house, which stood by the roadside; at the top of the meadow was a grove of fir trees, and at the bottom a running brook overhung by a steep bank.

While I was young I lived upon my mother's milk, as I could not eat grass. In the daytime I ran by her side, and at night I lay down close by her.

[…]

As soon as I was old enough to eat grass my mother used to go out to work in the daytime, and come back in the evening.

From *Black Beauty* by Anna Sewell

---

☞ **Answers and explanations on pages 124–126**

## SAMPLE TEST

---

**TEXT C**

'Why are you crying?'

'I was thinking,' said Dot.

'Oh! don't think!' pleaded the Kangaroo; 'I never do myself.'

'I can't help it!' explained the little girl. 'What do you do instead?' she asked.

'I always jump to conclusions,' said the Kangaroo, and she promptly bounded ten feet at one hop.

[…]

'Dear Kangaroo,' said Dot, 'do you know where I can get some water? I'm very thirsty!'

'Of course you are,' said her friend; 'everyone is at sundown. I'm thirsty myself. But the nearest water-hole is a longish way off, so we had better start at once.'

Little Dot got up with an effort. After her long run and fatigue, she was very stiff, and her little legs were so tired and weak, that after a few steps she staggered and fell.

[…]

'Just step into my pouch, and I'll hop you down to the water-hole in less time than it takes a locust to shrill.'

From *Dot and the Kangaroo* by Ethel C Pedley

---

**TEXT D**

'Quack?' said Jemima Puddle-duck, with her head and her bonnet on one side—'Quack?'

The gentleman raised his eyes above his newspaper and looked curiously at Jemima—

'Madam, have you lost your way?' said he. He had a long bushy tail which he was sitting upon, as the stump was somewhat damp.

Jemima thought him mighty civil and handsome. She explained that she had not lost her way, but that she was trying to find a convenient dry nesting-place.

'Ah! is that so? indeed!' said the gentleman with sandy whiskers, looking curiously at Jemima. …

I have a sackful of feathers in my wood-shed. No, my dear madam, you will be in nobody's way. You may sit there as long as you like,' said the bushy long-tailed gentleman.

From *The Tale of Jemima Puddle-Duck* by Beatrix Potter

## SAMPLE TEST

**1** A window cleaner is standing on the middle rung of a ladder washing windows. He climbs up 4 rungs to the next set of windows, then he sees one he has missed and goes back down 6 rungs. Following that he climbs up 8 rungs to wash the rest, then 5 more rungs to the top of the ladder. How many rungs does the ladder have?

A 23   B 25   C 21   D 24

**2** Kahliah and Max are watching an elderly man in a motorised wheelchair in a shop purchasing newspapers. The shopkeeper is speaking loudly and clearly to him. Kahliah and Max cannot hear what the elderly man is saying.

**Kahliah:** 'That old man must have dementia. She's talking to him like he's a child.'

What assumption has Kahliah made?

A You talk to a person with dementia like you would talk to a child.

B The shopkeeper speaks to all elderly people in that manner.

C The shopkeeper speaks to people in wheelchairs like you would talk to a child.

D The shopkeeper knows her customer and his capabilities.

**3** A piece was mistakenly cut from this cloth. Luckily there is some material available to patch it.

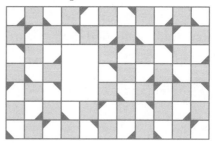

Which piece will match the pattern?

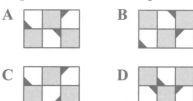

**4** When orchards and fields are filled with ripe crops and hired workers are in short supply or it's too expensive to harvest the crop and truck it to the wholesalers, it's cheaper to let the crops rot in the fields. Some farmers have been innovative and able to become involved in agritourism. Among other things, agritourism is a way to harvest farm produce, avoid waste and lend support to local communities through the economic benefits of tourism. Tourists travel to the farm, pay a fee, then pick and collect their own fruit and vegetables.

Which one of the following statements, if true, most **strengthens** the above argument?

A Agritourism involves a day trip to the countryside for urban dwellers.

B Agritourism is a win for the farmers, preventing wastage, and a win for people wanting fresh produce.

C Agritourism is a billion-dollar industry in Australia.

D Concern about the cost of insuring farm visitors in case of an accident deters some farmers from becoming involved in agritourism.

☞ **Answers and explanations on pages 126–129**

## SAMPLE TEST

**5** A Tsunami Detection and Early Warning System has been set up in the Philippines so that coastal communities can be evacuated in time and lives saved. Offshore ultrasonic tide-gauge sensors detect any sudden changes in sea level. Data is sent instantly to the receiving station on land. If an earthquake is strong enough to cause a tsunami warning, sirens alert communities to evacuate to higher ground. The further out to sea the earthquake, the more time communities have to evacuate. The sirens can also be used to warn about other disasters such as typhoons, flash floods and landslides but sometimes these are too sudden for advance warning.

If the information in the box is true, whose reasoning is **incorrect**?

A **Lottie:** 'When the siren is sounding, it doesn't necessarily mean a tsunami is coming.'

B **Ryan:** 'Just because the siren isn't sounding, it doesn't mean there isn't the potential for a sudden natural disaster.'

C **Emma:** 'When you don't hear the siren it means you don't have to be concerned at all about natural disasters.'

D **Fergus:** 'Sudden natural disasters such as landslides might not be predicted so the alarm system won't always work to save lives in those situations.'

**6** A gymnastic club has 162 members. All but 15 won medals at a recent competition. Four members won three medals each but nobody won more than 3. Altogether the members of the club won 213 medals. How many won 2 medals?

A 85

B 73

C 70

D 58

**7** Isla, Rhiannon and Petria play a game. They begin with 25 marbles each and take turns to spin this spinner.

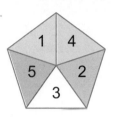

If they spin an even number, they receive two marbles from each of the others but, if they spin an odd number, they must give one marble to each of the others.

After all three girls have spun once, Rhiannon has 31 marbles. How many marbles will Petria have?

A 31      B 26      C 22      D 18

**8** Australia has the worst mammal extinction rate in the entire world partly due to European foxes, feral cats and wild dogs. These predator animals have almost caused the extinction of the brush-tailed bettong, the bilby and numerous other small mammals. Hope for the survival of the native species lies in the success of designated fenced areas that can be kept predator free. Small mammals can be safely reintroduced to the fenced predator-free areas once these areas have been cleared of feral predators.

Based on the above information, which conclusion must be true?

A While feral foxes and cats roam in the environment it's not safe there for small native mammals.

B Foxes and cats have almost caused the extinction of the brush-tailed bettong, the bilby and numerous other small mammals.

C Predator-free areas are fenced with 1.8-metre wire mesh designed to exclude foxes, cats and rabbits.

D The fences have access gates for rangers, scientists and traditional owners.

☞ **Answers and explanations on pages 126–129**

**9** The Munga-Thirri–Simpson Desert National Park covers 17 million hectares of land spread across the borders of Queensland, South Australia and the Northern Territory. It has the world's longest parallel sand dunes, some as high as 40 metres and extending for 200 kilometres, which formed 80 000 years ago. A surprising amount of specialised plant and animal life exists between the dunes in acacia shrub lands and spinifex grasslands. It is a globally significant region that should be protected for the future.

Which of the following statements most **strengthens** the above argument?

A The region's continuous First Nations custodianship stretches back thousands of years.

B The Munga-Thirri–Simpson Desert National Park is located near Australia's largest salt lake, Kati Thanda–Lake Eyre.

C When it rains in the Munga-Thirri, the temporary wetlands abound with bird life and native flowers.

D Fossil-fuel exploration would threaten this fragile desert environment and risk contamination of underground water resources, including the Great Artesian Basin.

**10** Five friends took part in a fun run.

- Keely and Victoria finished at the same time.
- Jackson finished 15 minutes after Victoria.
- Theo finished 10 minutes before Keely.
- Mia finished after Keely but before Jackson.
- The longest time any of them took was 55 minutes.

If all the above statements are true, only one of the sentences below might not be true. Which one is that?

A Jackson finished last.

B Theo finished 25 minutes before Jackson.

C Keely finished in 40 minutes.

D Mia finished in 50 minutes.

**11** Maria counted the number of dogs of different breeds that she saw at the park one day. She drew a graph of her results but forgot to label it.

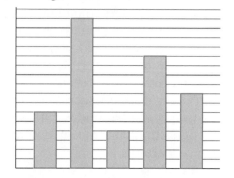

Maria remembers there were more labradors than any other breed and the number of labradors was equal to the total of chihuahuas and terriers. There were exactly half as many poodles as terriers. The other breed she saw was kelpies.

Which of these statements is **not** correct?

A The least number of dogs Maria saw was of chihuahuas.

B There were more kelpies than terriers.

C There were half as many kelpies as labradors.

D Together there were the same number of kelpies and terriers as there were of labradors and chihuahuas.

**12** Rhonda appeared in a play. The play was first performed on Wednesday 1 September and the last show was on 30 September. There were two performances every Saturday and Sunday and one every other day of the week except for Monday. Rhonda was unwell and did not appear on 17, 18 or 19 September.

In how many shows did Rhonda appear?

A 29        B 30        C 31        D 32

☞ **Answers and explanations on pages 126–129**

**13** Influenza (the flu) is caused by a group of respiratory viruses, which vary slightly from year to year so you need a new flu vaccination every year. Outbreaks usually occur over winter and as many as 5–20% of the population is affected. Influenza can lead to health complications such as bronchitis and is deadly in some cases, particularly for the elderly or frail. Vaccination offers a high level of protection. A flu vaccine is made from either inactivated or dead viruses, or only a single protein from a virus. These prompt your immune system to prepare for the virus. This takes about two weeks and then the vaccine will have an effect. A flu vaccination cannot give you the flu.

A **Simon:** 'I had the latest flu vaccine and then I got the flu. I was sneezing and I felt awful. I must have caught it just before my vaccination became effective. What bad luck.'

B **Beth:** 'If you get sick after a flu vaccine it's just coincidental because you must have caught a cold. The flu vaccine only protects against the flu.'

C **Assaf:** 'You can't catch the flu from a vaccination because the virus in the vaccine is inactivated.'

D **Ruth:** 'I was fully vaccinated two winters ago against the flu but it didn't work because I got the flu last winter.'

Which of the people above has made a mistake?

A  Simon          B  Beth

C  Assaf          D  Ruth

**14** The school held a competition to name the new arts building. The five top names were The Albert Namatjira Building, The Sally Gabori Building, The Ricky Maynard Building, The Minnie Pwerle Building and The Tracey Moffatt Building.

When the school community had a chance to vote, it was found that Minnie Pwerle was a more popular name for the arts building than Ricky Maynard. Everyone preferred Ricky Maynard to Tracey Moffatt. Albert Namatjira was more popular than Sally Gabori and Tracey Moffatt was preferred to Albert Namatjira and Sally Gabori.

Who was the building named after?

A  Ricky Maynard

B  Minnie Pwerle

C  Albert Namatjira

D  Tracey Moffatt

**15** Anton said that horseriding is a dangerous activity because you can fall off or be thrown by the horse and get badly hurt. He said that, on average, five people per year die in Australia as a result of a fall from a horse and that people simply don't understand the dangers of horseriding.

Which statement below most **weakens** Anton's argument?

A  A great many Australians enjoy horseriding for leisure or to engage in equestrian sporting events.

B  Horseriding can be good for the wellbeing of the rider, as proven by the Riding for the Disabled Association.

C  Horses can experience discomfort at being ridden and can buck to dislodge a rider.

D  People can reduce the risk of injury when horseriding by wearing protective clothing, learning about horse behaviour and improving their ability as a rider.

☞ **Answers and explanations on pages 126–129**

## SAMPLE TEST

**16** Two women (Natasha and Kyla) and three men (Akram, Anthony and Xavier) have stations next to each other at Natasha's nursery, as shown by the diagram. They each deal with one of the following: native plants, flowers, vegetables, grasses and garden equipment. One surname is Smith.

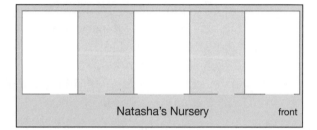

Natasha's Nursery                              front

These facts are known:

- Mr Armstrong deals with grasses. His station is next to Xavier's, which is the furthest from the front.
- The person in charge of vegetables is stationed next to Ms Watson.
- Akram Elomar is not the person who has native plants, who is stationed closest to the front.
- Ms Kwon has the centre station.
- Natasha used to deal with the flowers but that is now the work of another person so Natasha handles the garden equipment.

Who now works with the flowers?

A  Akram          B  Anthony
C  Kyla           D  Xavier

**17** Sally believed she had trained her pup Wilson to sit. Her brother decided to test Sally's belief and used this table.

| Time | Wilson told to sit | Wilson sat |
|------|--------------------|------------|
| 1    | Yes                | P          |
| 2    | No                 | Q          |
| 3    | R                  | No         |
| 4    | S                  | Yes        |

Which of the missing results are needed to determine whether the pup is properly trained to sit when told?

A  P and Q

B  P and R

C  P and S

D  Q and R

**18**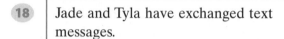
Jade and Tyla have exchanged text messages.

**Jade:** 'I'll drive up to visit you on Saturday. Can't wait to see your new house.'

**Tyla:** 'When you drive into town there's a big shopping centre on the left. Turn right there and my house is the white one halfway down the block on the left-hand side.'

What is Tyla's assumption?

A  Tyla has assumed which road Jade will use to enter town.

B  Tyla has assumed that Jade will be coming by car.

C  Tyla has assumed what time Jade will arrive.

D  Tyla has assumed that Jade is interested in seeing the house.

☞ **Answers and explanations on pages 126–129**

**19** 'Whoever left the gate open and allowed the kangaroos onto the lawn must have had both an opportunity and a motive.'

If this is true, which one of these sentences must also be true?

A If Craig had both an opportunity and a motive, he must have left the gate open.

B If Craig did not leave the gate open, he must not have had an opportunity.

C If Craig did not leave the gate open, he must have forgotten the motive.

D If Craig did not have a motive, he cannot have left the gate open.

**20** Samara has presents for her children, Ali and Mo. She has hidden one of the presents in one of three boxes and written two sentences on each box. At least one of those two sentences is true.

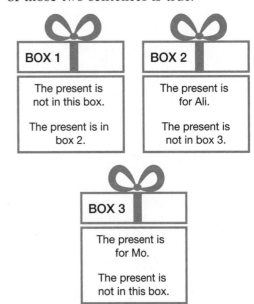

BOX 1

The present is not in this box.

The present is in box 2.

BOX 2

The present is for Ali.

The present is not in box 3.

BOX 3

The present is for Mo.

The present is not in this box.

Which must be true about the present?

A It is for Ali.

B It is for Mo.

C It is in box 2.

D It is in box 3.

☞ **Answers and explanations on pages 126–129**

# SAMPLE TEST

**1** How many blocks would be needed, using the same pattern, to add one more layer at the bottom of this object?

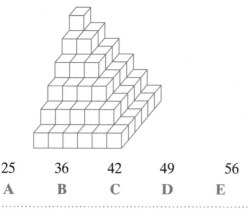

| 25 | 36 | 42 | 49 | 56 |
|----|----|----|----|----|
| A | B | C | D | E |

**2** Sean's age next year is a multiple of 5. The year after it will be a multiple of 7. How old might he be now?

| 4 | 9 | 19 | 24 | 34 |
|---|---|----|----|----|
| A | B | C | D | E |

**3** Zeke is making this design, which has one line of symmetry.

He wants the design to be accurate and is using a protractor as he forms the angles. He has only completed part of the design.

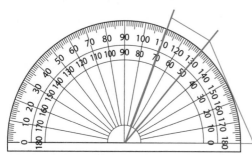

What will be the size of the shaded angle?

| 100° | 110° | 120° | 130° | 140° |
|------|------|------|------|------|
| A | B | C | D | E |

**4** Billy rolls a dice.

Which statements are correct?

**1** The probability that Billy rolls 5 is $\frac{1}{5}$.

**2** The probability that Billy rolls an even number is $\frac{1}{2}$.

**3** The probability that Billy rolls a number less than 3 is $\frac{1}{3}$.

A all of them
B 1 and 2 only
C 1 and 3 only
D 2 and 3 only
E none of them

**5** Every row, every column and both diagonals of this magic square add to the same amount. What number should go where the **X** is?

| 30 |    | 44 | X  |
|----|----|----|----|
| 41 | 36 | 35 | 38 |
| 37 |    |    | 34 |
|    |    | 32 |    |

| 33 | 39 | 40 | 42 | 45 |
|----|----|----|----|----|
| A | B | C | D | E |

**6** Cathy runs round the oval in 50 seconds whereas it takes Freddy 1 minute and 20 seconds. How many complete laps will Cathy have run when Freddie drops out exhausted after 6 laps?

| 8 | 9 | 10 | 11 | 12 |
|---|---|----|----|----|
| A | B | C | D | E |

☞ **Answers and explanations on pages 129–130**

## SAMPLE TEST

**7** Two circles, one with radius 2 cm and one with radius 3 cm, are next to each other in a rectangle as shown in the diagram.

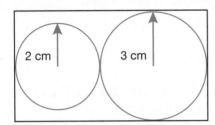

What is the area of the rectangle?

| 15 cm² | 30 cm² | 45 cm² | 50 cm² | 60 cm² |
|--------|--------|--------|--------|--------|
| A | B | C | D | E |

**8** I pay $6 060 for a motorboat and a trailer. If the motorboat cost four times as much as the trailer, how much was the trailer?

| $1015 | $1212 | $756 | $1010 | $1515 |
|-------|-------|------|-------|-------|
| A | B | C | D | E |

**9** A snail starts at the spot marked X. Which side of this regular pentagon will it be on after crawling 0.65 of the distance around the outside of the pentagon in a clockwise direction?

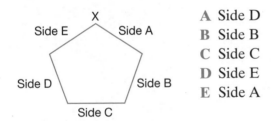

A  Side D
B  Side B
C  Side C
D  Side E
E  Side A

**10** Sally's parents take an 8:30 am flight from Sydney to Perth. The flight takes $4\frac{3}{4}$ hours. Given that the time in Perth is 2 hours behind Sydney's time, and allowing 45 minutes for luggage collection and travel, when will they reach their hotel, Perth time?

A  2:00 pm
B  12:45 am
C  12 noon
D  11:45 am
E  1:15 pm

**11** Two children were making propellers for their toy plane. They put a number on one blade of the propeller, then turned it round 180° and wrote the same number. They were surprised to find that both looked the same.

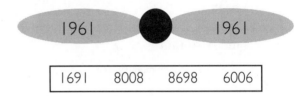

| 1691 | 8008 | 8698 | 6006 |
|------|------|------|------|

How many of the numbers in the box would have the same property?

| 0 | 1 | 2 | 3 | 4 |
|---|---|---|---|---|
| A | B | C | D | E |

**12** Five apples were cut into quarters. Zoe ate $\frac{3}{4}$ of an apple and Doug ate $1\frac{3}{4}$. Suzy ate $\frac{1}{2}$ an apple, Mel ate 1 apple and Yaz ate the rest.

Which of these statements are correct?

**1** Mel and Yaz ate the same amount.

**2** Zoe ate $\frac{1}{4}$ more than Suzy.

**3** Yaz ate twice as much as Suzy.

A  2 only
B  1 and 2 only
C  1 and 3 only
D  2 and 3 only
E  1, 2 and 3

**13** A parking area has spaces for 1000 vehicles. Two-fifths of the spaces are for trucks. Yesterday there were 200 trucks parked in the area and the car section was three-quarters full. How many cars were there in the parking area?

| 400 | 450 | 550 | 600 | 750 |
|-----|-----|-----|-----|-----|
| A | B | C | D | E |

☞ **Answers and explanations on pages 129–130**

**14** Here are three statements about the information in the graph:

**X** January had about one-quarter of the rainfall in March.

**Y** The difference between the rainfall in the wettest and driest months is about 6 cm.

**Z** Together May and June had about 1 metre of rain.

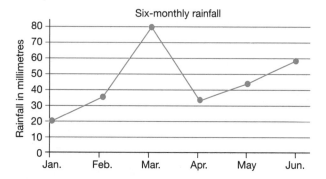

Six-monthly rainfall

Which of these statements are correct?

A X only
B X and Y only
C X and Z only
D Y and Z only
E X, Y and Z

**15** An express train which travels at 110 km per hour leaves Sydney (S) at 7 am to travel to Melbourne (M). At the same time a goods train, which travels at 55 km per hour, leaves Melbourne bound for Sydney. The goods train has to make a number of detours.

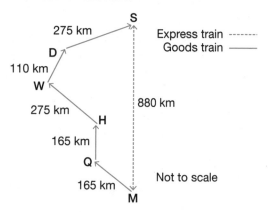

Where will the goods train be when the express train is halfway to Melbourne?
A between Q and H
B between H and W
C at W
D at H
E at Q

**16** Thirty-nine people bought a total of 64 ice creams from a stall. Six people bought three ice creams each and the rest bought either one or two.

How many people bought exactly one ice cream?

| 13 | 15 | 18 | 20 | 21 |
|----|----|----|----|----|
| A  | B  | C  | D  | E  |

**17** Ned mixed lemonade and passionfruit nectar to make the quantity of drink shown in the jug.

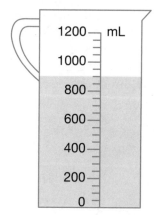

If there is five times as much lemonade as nectar, how much passionfruit nectar did Ned use?
A 100 mL
B 125 mL
C 150 mL
D 175 mL
E 180 mL

☞ **Answers and explanations on pages 129–130**

**18** Here are the first six terms in a pattern, although two numbers were too hard to read and so they now say P and Q.

2, P, 7, Q, 12, 13

The rule for each number in the pattern (after the first 3) is to use the three numbers just before it. The two numbers just before the number are added and the number before those two numbers is subtracted. So to find the number for Q, P and 7 would be added and then 2 taken away.

What will the seventh number in the pattern be?

| 8 | 14 | 15 | 16 | 17 |
|---|----|----|----|----|
| A | B | C | D | E |

**19** Pat has been laying pavers. He begins with this pattern. It has a perimeter of 1.44 m.

Pat wants his pattern to be bigger so he adds two pavers at the top and two at the bottom.

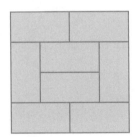

The perimeter is now 1.92 m.

How wide are the pavers?

| 8 cm | 9 cm | 10 cm | 12 cm | 15 cm |
|------|------|-------|-------|-------|
| A | B | C | D | E |

**20** In a competition, players are awarded ribbons. The ribbons are either green or blue and each colour is worth a certain number of points, the same number each time.

Maxine earned 5 blue and 8 green ribbons and got 44 points.

Xavier earned 7 blue and 10 green ribbons and got 58 points.

How many points is a green ribbon worth?

| 1 | 2 | 3 | 4 | 5 |
|---|---|---|---|---|
| A | B | C | D | E |

☞ **Answers and explanations on pages 129–130**

# Introduction

In both the Writing Test of the NSW Selective High School Placement Test and the Written Expression Test of the ACER Scholarship Tests (Secondary Level 1), there is a strong emphasis on quality above quantity in judging the worth of an essay.

The types of texts covered in the NSW Education Standards Authority English K–6 Modules are: narrative, recount (literary or factual), information report, procedure, explanation, discussion, exposition, description (literary or factual), poetry and response.

In the tests, candidates may choose whichever type of text they wish, though the stimulus material will more often than not dictate which type or types would be most suitable (e.g. 'Write a story ...'; 'Use this illustration ...'; 'You could write a story, a description or a discussion ...'). Within these limits a candidate is best advised to choose the type of text that suits their particular strengths. The types most likely to be relevant to this kind of test are: narrative, description (literary or factual), recount, discussion and exposition. We will concentrate on these types of texts.

Practise! Writing is no different from any other skill. The more often it is practised, the better it will become—always provided due attention is given to quality!

Every time students write a review, a narrative, a piece of information, a poem or any form of writing in any subject in their own words, they should attempt o develop greater expertise. Whatever the exercise it is an opportunity to improve in fluency, coherence and vocabulary—and, indirectly, to practise for tests. It is essential that quality—and, hopefully, enjoyment—is always at the forefront of their minds.

## Writing for a test

Impromptu writing tests (that is, where there is no time for research and little time to prepare, plan or proofread) are challenging so speed of thought and writing becomes vital. As candidates are given only 25 or 30 minutes for each piece of writing the following procedure is recommended:

### Preparation

As soon as the test starts, take up to five minutes to:

- read the question **carefully**—the stimulus material, or prompt, may take either a verbal or picture form—or a combination of the two
- if there is a choice, decide on your subject
- if there is a choice, decide on your type of text.

### Brainstorming

- Jot down any and all ideas that come into your head on the topic.
- Use a mind map or notes to link your ideas together.
- Discard any ideas that are not relevant to the exercise.
- Organise your thoughts into a coherent order. (Note the 'five-paragraph essay' format below.)
- Start writing.

Don't panic if you see those around you writing frantically from the word go. The extra purpose and direction you will gain from your 'pre-writing' planning will prove worthwhile.

## Introduction

### The writing process

It is a considerable advantage to have some ready-made and familiar format at one's fingertips, not only from the point of view of time but, perhaps even more importantly, of confidence. The **five-paragraph essay** form can be useful. It can help a great deal in developing the speed, coherence and conciseness that are so important in tests of this kind.

It need not, of course, be precisely **five** paragraphs. In a discussion text, for example, when you may be giving two (or more) sides to an argument, you may choose to allocate equal paragraphs to each side thus making four, six or even more paragraphs more suitable. However, in the time allotted, five paragraphs will generally prove suitable for the exercise: an introduction, three supporting paragraphs to develop your approach to the topic in depth, then another to close.

### Proofreading

If you have time, quickly check your work to eliminate spelling mistakes and other errors.

## The five-paragraph essay

1  Introduction
2  First supporting paragraph
3  Second supporting paragraph
4  Third supporting paragraph
5  Conclusion

### Paragraphs

The usual format for a paragraph is to start with a topic sentence (what the paragraph is to be about) followed by supporting sentences which back up the topic sentence, then end with a strong final sentence. The next paragraph should follow on as naturally as possible from the one before and from the introduction.

### Adapted for narratives and literary recounts (retelling a story)

1  Introduction (introduces the main character(s) and setting)
2  First supporting paragraph (a change or disruption that disturbs the state of affairs)
3  Second supporting paragraph (develops the 'problems' of the preceding paragraph, perhaps towards a climax)
4  Third supporting paragraph (begins to resolve the 'problems' being encountered or reaches a climax)
5  Conclusion (finally resolves the problem and, perhaps, adds character development as a result of the experience)

A 25- or 30-minute test is not really enough time in which to do credit to a short story. There is neither time nor space to develop a character and a plot, including some kind of conflict and resolution, in sufficient depth to properly showcase a writer's skills. It is better to limit yourself to something less ambitious, such as a description, discussion or exposition, and do it with depth and style.

The example below is 400 words, which is longer than would be expected in a 25- or 30-minute test.

# Narrative

## Example of a narrative

---

### Topic—A family tale

I was coming home from school when I heard the news that my dad's shop had been vandalised by some teenagers. When I arrived home I heard my dad arguing with my mum about whether we should leave the country or not. I agreed with my dad who wanted us to leave, especially after the taunts I had had to endure over the past few weeks. I definitely knew what the other members of the family wanted to do. We had been called 'stupid Jews' throughout our neighbourhood. *(introduction—main character and background presented)*

It didn't help that we were poor and living in a two-bedroom house in a Warsaw ghetto. With three brothers and a baby sister, our home was very crowded. It really didn't help, either, that our dad was getting drunk more and more often although it wasn't hard to understand why. On top of all his personal worries, there were strong rumours of the Germans invading Poland. *(development of the plot—further complications)*

The night of 17 June 1938 was a night I hope one day to forget. It was the night the bombs began to shower down on the quiet streets of Warsaw, my city. I woke up in the middle of the night, at first not understanding what the violent shrieks and explosions were. Our whole family was terrified and, to make it worse, Dad had been arrested earlier in the night for being drunk. Mum and the rest of us clung together and, panicking, we rushed outside and ran through the dark alleyways, trying to flee from the horror that rained down on us from above. As we turned a corner, I heard an explosion close behind us and, whirling round, I saw the home I was born in disintegrate like so many matchsticks. *(further development—with the complications reaching a climax)*

As we neared the railway station, we were stopped by a soldier, a soldier I suddenly realised was a German. My mother handed the baby to me and screamed, 'Run!' We ran. The soldier let us go without a glance but led my mother away. *(the climax—it can't get much worse)*

We ran to the station, longing just to escape. But so did the rest of the city. Our baby sister was crying in my arms. Even she could see the fear and anxiety on my face. We prayed for our parents. We didn't know where they were or where the train was going or what lay ahead of us. But, most of all, we prayed the Germans wouldn't be there. *(a form of resolution although in this example, we are left 'hanging', with the implication it is just the end of a chapter)*

Based on *A Family Tale* by Caden Wilkinson, aged 12

---

# Factual recount

**Factual recount**

1  Introduction (the who, where and when)

2  First supporting paragraph (the start of a chronological record of events)

3  Second supporting paragraph (a continuation or further step in the record of events)

4  Third supporting paragraph (evaluative comments—these can also be made during the record of events)

5  Conclusion (rounding off the retelling with an effective point).

## Example of a factual recount

See below for description—the planning and execution are similar for both.

**Description** (this can  be a person, place or object)

1  Introduction (present the subject)

2  First supporting paragraph (physical characteristics, qualities and background)

3  Second supporting paragraph (development, special or notable features)

4  Third supporting paragraph (the most significant attribute or development)

5  Conclusion (round off with an effective point)

## An example of preparation

Topic: The Telephone (The stimulus question may be a picture or a word.)

**Brainstorming**

Communication, tele means far off, phone means hear, whistles, drums, smoke signals, flags, AG Bell, tins and wire, another room, public phones, one phone per house, overseas, telecommunications, computers, answering machines, mobiles, everybody has one, business, safety, peace of mind, cheap

**Mindmap** (in this case, organise chronologically)

And then—**write!**

## Factual recount

## Example of a factual recount (description)

### The telephone

The telephone has been perhaps the most significant invention of the past 150 years. Society had used various means to communicate to this point: smoke signals, whistles, mirrors, drums and flags for semaphore. Electricity meant that the time was ready for a far more sophisticated method. *(introduction—presents the subject)*

In 1876 Alexander Graham Bell, an American, produced the first machine that meant a speech sound (phone) could be heard at a distance (tele); in Bell's case, in another room. This original invention simply involved the use of a wire, magnets and an electric current. *(first supporting paragraph—physical characteristics, background)*

The world at that time *(link with preceding paragraph)* was astonished to be able to speak to others through an operator who directed the call. Eventually the public telephones gave way to a phone in some, most and then all homes. No longer was an operator necessary—it was all done automatically. And not just to someone else nearby. Our world shrank so that anyone could communicate, almost immediately, with someone else in the most far-flung reaches on earth. *(second supporting paragraph—special features and development; in this case, chronologically)*

Now, of course, *(link with preceding paragraph)* we have ceased to marvel at the machine. Rather we have come to complain bitterly when something prevents us using the offshoots it has produced: the fax, the answering machine, email and the internet. *(third supporting paragraph—chronological development to present day and full significance)*

There is no doubting *(link phrase)* that the telephone, from its simple beginnings, has led to huge businesses in this age of telecommunications; so huge that this area is now the fastest-growing industry in the world. But perhaps even more significant than the emergence of these huge corporations, there is the tiny mobile phone. Its professional value aside, the invention of the telephone, by the fact that we can now so easily keep in touch with loved ones and verify their wellbeing and safety, has meant more to most of us than the huge quantities of money all the big businesses of the world together can produce. *(conclusion—round off effectively)*

# Discussion

**Discussion** (present two sides to an argument; four or six paragraphs may suit better)

**1** Introduction (present person, place or thing to be discussed)

**2** First supporting paragraph (side 1)

**3** Second supporting paragraph (side 1)

**4** First supporting paragraph (side 2)

**5** Second supporting paragraph (side 2)

**6** Conclusion (sum up, usually in favour of one side)

**Note:** If there are more than two items to be discussed, it would be wise to confine the presentations to only one paragraph per item to keep the comparisons within manageable limits for the time frame involved).

**Example of a discussion:** *Topic—Should homework be given to primary-school children?*

*Brainstorm:* study habits, ~~otherwise be watching TV~~, no time to play outside, tired after working all day, reinforce school learning, limited amount OK, bridge between school and home, turn off any love of learning, ~~homework is good for you~~, ~~is old fashioned~~ (*points crossed out discarded as too weak*)

Mindmap and organise

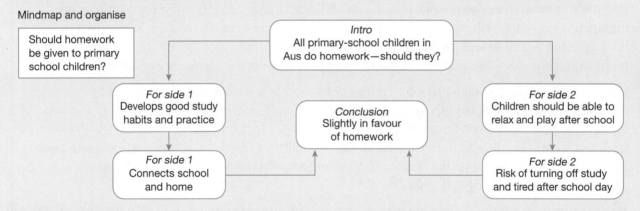

And then—**write!**

Again note that this is only an example (380 words) and more time was spent on it than 25 to 30 minutes. The example gives you an idea of the type of text (a discussion) in use, both in preparation and the finished article.

## *Discussion*

### Example of a discussion

> **Discussion:** *Should homework be given to primary-school children?*
>
> The matter for discussion is whether primary-age children should have to do homework. Almost all schools set homework for this age group but there is some argument against it. (*introduction — the matter to be discussed*)
>
> Firstly (*link with preceding paragraph*) we will discuss the arguments for having homework (*paragraph topic sentence*). As most students are about to embark on a long learning cycle which will take them from age 7 to age 22 or 24 for many, the sooner they develop sound study habits, the better. This need not be a long stint to start with, just a short piece of written work, perhaps with some learning such as spelling, at a certain time each afternoon. At the same time it can be used as reinforcement of some lessons learnt at school that day. (*first supporting paragraph, side 1*)
>
> Secondly (*link with preceding paragraph*) it is good for parents to see their child working at home (*paragraph topic sentence*). On the one hand, they see how their child approaches work and on the other hand they see what work is being done. Without this, parents often have little or no understanding of the syllabus or how it is being taught by their child's teacher. Similarly it is healthy for the child to experience their parents' interest in their schoolwork. In this way homework provides a bridge between school and home. (*second supporting paragraph, side 1*)
>
> On the other hand (*link with preceding paragraph*) there is a strong case put forward by opponents of homework for this age group (*paragraph topic sentence*). Time after school should be time for healthy, enjoyable, childish pursuits such as outdoor games, hobbies and the like. Children should be allowed to relax without the thought of even more schoolwork hanging over them, especially as the work, the hours and 'keeping up with the others' has usually meant a tiring day. (*first supporting paragraph, side 2*)
>
> Besides this (*link with preceding paragraph*), the risk of turning young minds off a love of learning at such a young age is a very real one (*paragraph topic sentence*). Forcing them back to their school books after a full school day could easily make this time a grind to be dreaded each afternoon. (*second supporting paragraph, side 2*)
>
> All in all (*link with preceding paragraphs*), the points made by the affirmative (those for homework) side do seem slightly stronger, with the proviso that the length of time be limited, both by the age of the child and by the speed at which the individual child can work. (*conclusion — summing up and resolving the argument*)

# Exposition

**Exposition** (used to argue a case for or against a particular point of view)

1   Introduction (presents point of view to be argued)

2   First supporting paragraph (first point supporting your argument plus details or examples)

3   Second supporting paragraph (second point supporting your argument plus details or examples)

4   Third supporting paragraph (third point supporting your argument plus details or examples)

5   Conclusion (round off, assert your viewpoint forcefully as a result of the points made in the three supporting paragraphs)

## Example of an exposition

Friends, let me conclude by pointing out all those very real and sensible reasons you should be making sure I am your selected candidate next Saturday. *(introduction—states point of view)*

Firstly all my priorities are linked with this area of the state *(topic sentence for paragraph 2)*. I live here, my family lives here and we have lived here for years. In fact, I am a true-blue product of my area. That's more than you can say for any of my opponents! They seem to believe they can just walk in here, without anyone in the district having known them for more than a few months, no, make that weeks, and expect to raise the support needed to win OUR seat. What a hide! They are asking all of you to accept them at face value, without establishing any of the reputation for honesty and integrity that I have managed to do. *(supporting paragraph 1—with supporting points)*

Secondly I am a man of the people *(paragraph topic sentence)*. I haven't gone off and got some kind of fancy degree from a city university. I haven't wasted my time getting meaningless letters after my name, just to impress everyone. I have just plugged away, among you and with you, while we try our hardest to make what we can of this land and this community. OUR land and OUR community, that is. And that's what I'll continue to do, to the very best of my ability, after I become your chosen representative next Saturday. *(supporting paragraph 2—with supporting points)*

And finally, my friends, my very good friends, and most importantly, after you have selected me, you won't find me spending my time, and your money, lapping up the luxuries Sydney has to offer or enjoying expensive junkets abroad *(paragraph topic sentence)*. I'll be here, available to hear your problems, to listen to what is needed, to help as best I can in making our area without peer in this great state. *(supporting paragraph 3—with supporting points)*

So it's up to you! My name will be there on the ballot papers in the election and I have every confidence that these very strong arguments I have presented to you here today have convinced you it's my name you'll be putting a big '1' next to, come Saturday. Thank you very much for giving me your time today, my friends. I wish you all the very best for the future; a future that will, hopefully, see me helping you to the very best of my ability to make the most we can of our own wellbeing and that of our community. *(conclusion—a powerful restatement of the theme)*

# Report

**Report** (used to provide information to be shared)

## Introduction

- The first paragraph succinctly introduces the subject of the report and provides new or interesting information for the reader. It may also include a brief description.
- Report topics focus on people, places or things—living and non-living.
- Reports can be grouped into three broad types:
  - o scientific reports that focus on the appearance and behaviour of the report subject
  - o technological reports that examine the components and the application of scientific knowledge
  - o social reports that examine aspects of society through descriptions of people, places, history, geography, the arts and government.

## Subsequent and supporting paragraphs

- Supporting paragraphs provide factual information about the subject using the correct technical and scientific terms. Definitions are used, if necessary, to avoid reader confusion—they help organise and elaborate on the subject.
- Subsequent paragraphs fundamentally focus on single important ideas or concepts. They are introduced by a topic sentence.
- Reports are written in the present tense.
- Reports are written from a third-person perspective. Personal pronouns such as *I, we, our* and *my* do not feature in reports. Reports are to remain objective.
- Report information avoids emotive language or personal opinions. There are restricted opportunities for figurative language. Comparative language (smaller, similar to, brighter) is useful to improve clarity of writing.

## Conclusion

The concluding paragraph:

- focuses on what the reader has learnt from the report. It briefly restates the critical points or issues contained in the report
- includes an optional rounding off with a general statement about the topic
- includes a short sentence that takes the reader back to the opening paragraph
- does not include any new information
- is short and to the point to drive home awareness of the issue or topic addressed in the report.

## *Report*

## Example of a report

### Carlo Sandblow

A sign on a low lookout to Carlo Sandblow describes the area as 'a sea of sand creeping slowly inland'. Vast masses of such sand constitute both Fraser Island and the Cooloola coastline. The sand masses account for well over half of the Great Sandy Region's 350 000 hectares. *(introduction: presents the subject)*

However, in time new sandblows will overlap older, revegetated blows to build the dunes up to great heights above sea level, some becoming the highest sand dunes in the world. Sand dunes are places of constant change and movement. *(additional supporting paragraph: basic overview of the features)*

Sandblows in this area are created by strong onshore winds from the south-east picking up grains of sand and carrying them inland, eventually smothering the vegetation cover. Over thousands of years of sandblow development, plants eventually recolonise and stabilise the exposed sands. One of the most accessible sandblows is the Carlo Sandblow near Rainbow Beach in Queensland. *(second supporting paragraph: general overview)*

Most of the sand on the Cooloola coast and Fraser Island originally came from New South Wales. Scientists have discovered that a vast amount of it once filled what are now deep valleys of the Blue Mountains. The heavy rains falling on the eastern side of the Great Dividing Range has eroded away the sedimentary rocks and granites which chiefly comprise the mountains to the west of the coastal plains. The resulting sand is carried down to the sea to meet the next agent of transport — the sea — at the river mouth. The beaches have for millions of years been fed by the continual flow of sand down the rivers. *(third supporting paragraph: geological explanation for this specific example)*

The sand of The Great Sandy Region has accumulated and been deposited during the last two million years. The sand has had a long, interesting history of movement. It was initially solid rock, broken down by erosion and weathering to grains which are so small and so light they can be blown about by the wind. The sand is moved along the coast by wave action, wind and currents. *(fourth paragraph: supporting specific geological explanation)*

Carlo Sandblow is a sand mass covering over 15 hectares and part of the Cooloola sand mass. It is one of the largest accumulations of wind-blown sand found along Queensland's coastline. It is a unique 'moonscape' sand mass and overlooks the towering, coloured sand cliffs and the coastline north to Inskip Peninsula near the southern tip of Fraser Island. *(fourth supporting paragraph: physical attributes and appearance)*

This sandblow was named in 1770 by Captain Cook after Carlo, one of his deck hands when the *Endeavour* sailed up the Queensland coast. *(concluding paragraph: a historical fact effectively rounds off the text and redirects the reader to the introduction)*

## PRACTICE QUESTIONS

**1 B  2 B**  Page 3

1  Sarah fears her brother's habit of filling the house with animals and neglecting the needs of his human patients will lead them to poverty. The trend that has begun—four patients driven away—is alarming to her.

  **A is incorrect.** Sarah grumbles about his behaviour and sees nothing to admire in it.

  **C and D are incorrect.** Nothing about his behaviour arouses her curiosity (C) or makes her want to understand it (D).

2  Sarah uses the word personage rather than person to indicate these are people of some importance to Doctor Dolittle's medical practice.

  **A is incorrect.** There is no evidence that any of these people are famous.

  **C is incorrect.** The word does not refer to the age of the patients who have left Doctor Dolittle's practice. It is true that the lady with rheumatism is old but it does not follow that the others are also old.

  **D is incorrect.** Although these 'personages' are visitors in a sense, Sarah is drawing the Doctor's attention to the fact they are his valuable patients ('best people') and should be properly looked after by him.

**1 D  2 C**  Page 6

1  Matilda's lies were extremely dangerous so her punishment of missing out on a visit to the theatre is more than reasonable.

  **The other options are incorrect.** These answers suggest the punishment was unfair in some way and was greater than the crime deserved, which is clearly not the case.

2  No-one listens to Matilda's cries for help when there is a real fire so no-one comes to her aid. It is most likely (note the reference to 'increasing heat') the house will be burnt down on her Aunt's return.

  **A and B are incorrect.** People ignore Matilda's cries for help as she has lied so often in the past.

  **D is incorrect.** There is a real fire and if it isn't stopped, it is sure to damage the house.

**1 C  2 A  3 D**  Page 9

1  In the previous sentence the author states that nuns are given a new name when they enter a convent. The missing sentence tells the reader the name this nun was given and why it was chosen for her: The new name she was given, Sister Teresa, paid tribute to that of a saint (Saint Therese de Lisieux). The sentence following explains that her name was changed again when she took her final vows.

2  In the previous sentence the author says Mother Teresa set up an organisation called Missionaries of Charity to give help to those in need. The missing sentence explains who was identified as being in need for the Charity's purposes: This included orphaned children or those suffering from diseases such as leprosy and AIDS. The sentence that follows explains that Mother Teresa devoted the rest of her life to this cause.

3  In the previous sentence the author points out that 1979 was the year when the Nobel Committee had the children's suffering and refugees in mind when considering awarding Nobel prizes. The missing sentence notes that this was the year when Mother Teresa won a Nobel prize: It was in this year that Mother Teresa was awarded the Nobel Peace Prize. The sentence that follows claims her canonisation as a saint was another outcome of her selfless work for those in need.

  The unused sentence is B.

**1 B 2 A 3 B**  Page 12

1 Text B is a memoir made up almost entirely of personal memories. Text A is mainly a record of Henry Lawson's schooldays with two brief personal memories included.

2 Text A refers to Henry Lawson as 'the poet and short-story writer', which suggests he is a well-known figure in the community. There is no indication in Text B that the narrator, Pearl Jones, is well known.

3 Pearl Jones says children were tied by rope to the backs of their chairs to make them sit up straight, a practice that would not be allowed in today's schools. In Text A, although the classroom described is very different from a classroom of today, it does not refer to a method of discipline that currently would be frowned upon.

## YEAR 5 THINKING SKILLS

### PRACTICE QUESTIONS

**1 C 2 D 3 A 4 B**  Page 21

1 The argument is that the development application should be refused because the standing building is historically important to the area. The fact that a heritage report has stated the building is the last remaining example of inter-war architecture in the area most strengthens this argument.

**A is incorrect**. This statement about the area being in need of housing for low-income workers could be used to strengthen an argument against building the premium apartments but it does not strengthen the argument about the standing building being saved because of its historical importance.

**B is incorrect**. This statement about new retail outlets neither strengthens nor weakens the argument about the historical importance of the standing building, especially since the standing building already has shops.

**D is incorrect**. This statement about the height of the new development could be used to strengthen an argument against the new development but it does not strengthen the argument about the standing building being saved because of its historical importance.

2 The Principal's conclusion is that the team must win the debate. The evidence she bases this on is that if they don't win it will hurt the reputation of the school. For the principal's conclusion to hold, it must be assumed that students must not do anything to hurt the reputation of the school. (If we don't win the debate, it will hurt the reputation of the school + students must not do anything to hurt the reputation of the school means therefore we must win the debate.)

**A is incorrect**. This is the principal's conclusion, not an assumption she has made in order to reach a conclusion.

**B is incorrect**. This could be true. It could also be an assumption. However, it is not the assumption the principal made because it does not lead from the evidence to her conclusion. (If we don't win the debate, it will hurt the reputation of the school + the school debate team is not very strong does not mean therefore we must win the debate.)

**C is incorrect**. This could be true. It could also be an assumption. However, it is not the assumption the principal made because it does not lead from the evidence to her conclusion. (If we don't win the debate, it will hurt the reputation of the school + students get excited when their team wins does not mean therefore we must win the debate.)

3 We know any students who didn't get a chance to work in the kitchen garden last term will be selected to work there this term. However, that does not mean anyone who worked in the garden last term will definitely not be selected to work there again this term. So this sentence shows the flaw in Grace's reasoning: she may still be selected to work in the garden this term.

**B and C are incorrect**. These sentences are true and not a mistake made by Grace.

**D is incorrect.** This sentence is a mistake since the teacher said they definitely will be selected to work in the garden this term. It is not, however, a mistake made by Grace.

4  The information tells us that everyone in favour of selling eggs was also in favour of a raffle. And no-one who was in favour of a raffle was in favour of creating a book of recipes. So it is reasonable to draw the conclusion that if Liora is in favour of selling eggs, she does not want to create a recipe book.

**A and C are incorrect.** There is not enough information to draw these conclusions.

**D is incorrect.** The information tells us that everyone in favour of a raffle was also in favour of a quiz night but it does not follow that everyone in favour of a quiz night was also in favour of a raffle.

**1 C  2 B  3 C  4 D  5 A**    Page 24

1  Shape 2 has a different pattern, but shapes 1, 3 and 4 all have the same pattern in different orientations. Shape 1 would be the same as shape 3 if rotated 90° in an anticlockwise direction. Shape 1 would be the same as shape 4 if rotated 90° in a clockwise direction. Shapes 3 and 4 are the shapes that would be the same if either one was rotated 180°.

2  The tail at the end of the arrow points in the other direction.

3  The nets in 1 and 2 cannot form cubes. This will be seen if the nets are cut out and folded.

4  All four shapes can be formed.

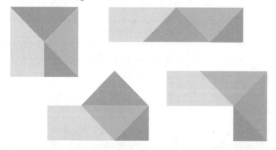

5  Imagine how the pieces could fit together. For example, notice that the top of the third piece will fit with either option A and option D, or twice with option B (which is one too

many times). None of the pieces will fit with the left side of option D.

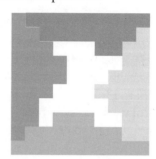

**1 D  2 A  3 B  4 A**    Page 26

1  The post office, newsagency and chemist are all east of the bank. The real-estate office is west of the bank, so it is furthest west with the bank next to it. The middle business is not the chemist (because there must be two businesses between it and the real-estate office) or the newsagency because that is not next to the bank. It must be the post office.

| Real estate | Bank | Post office | Chemist | Newsagency |
| --- | --- | --- | --- | --- |

2  Dean was last. Pedro finished before both Grant and Isaac and they both finished before Jonathan. So Pedro must have finished first. So the statement 'Pedro did not finish first' cannot be true. All the other options could be true.

3  Oliver is second. Arden, Imogen, Wendy and Cooper are all behind Sonia so Sonia must be first. This means that Arden must be third. Imogen is in front of Cooper and also Wendy as she is next to Cooper so Imogen is fourth. Wendy and Cooper are fifth and sixth in some order. A is false, C and D might or might not be true.

4  Millie and Willow live next door to each other. They each have just one brother meaning neither can live at number 3 so one must live at number 4, and the other at either 2 or 6. Aurelia and her sister also live next door to Willow. Because Millie has no sister

she must live at either 2 or 6, Willow must live at 4 and Aurelia and her sister at 6 or 2. Now, Rose has no siblings and, as she lives at one end of the close, she must live at either number 1 or number 5. Ophelia must then live at number 6 or number 2. So Ophelia is Aurelia's sister. Theo lives opposite Ophelia in a higher-numbered house than Rose so Ophelia must live at number 6. Millie lives at number 2.

**1 C  2 C  3 C  4 D  5 B  6 A**   Page 28

1  The highest total score from the first four rounds is 33 for Abdul. The next highest score is 30 for Ricky. The highest mark Ricky could score in round 5 is 10. So the highest score he can achieve after the final round is 40. If Abdul scores 41 or higher, he is guaranteed the outright win. Now, 41 – 33 = 8. The minimum score Abdul can get to be guaranteed the win is 8.

2  Four houses have three cars so the remaining 39 houses have either one or two cars. As 68 – 4 × 3 = 68 – 12 = 56, those 39 houses have 56 cars altogether. Now, 56 – 39 = 17. So there are 17 more cars than houses. This means that 17 houses have two cars. The number of houses with one car is 39 – 17 or 22.

3  There are four possibilities for the first person. For each of those possibilities there are three choices for the second person. For each of those possibilities there are two choices for the third person. Once those three positions are determined there is only one possibility for the final person. The number of ways is 4 × 3 × 2 × 1 = 24.

4  Veronica is taller than Ronald so is not the shortest. Both Lachlan and Zoe are taller than Veronica and Nathan is taller than Lachlan. So three people are taller than Veronica. She must be the second shortest. The other options might or might not be true. There is not enough information to determine whether they are true or not.

5  Try each option. 4 × 3 = 12. 12 + 8 = 20. 20 ÷ 2 = 10. 10 – 6 = 4.

6  The phone number is a seven-digit number and the last digit is 7. The two-digit number formed by the first two numbers is twice the two-digit number formed by the last two digits but half of the three-digit number formed by the middle three digits. So the two-digit number formed by the last two numbers must be less than 50 and the two-digit number formed by the first two numbers must be greater than 50.

So the last two digits can only be 27, 37 or 47.

If the last two digits are 27, the first two digits are 54 and the middle three digits are 108.

If the last two digits are 37, the first two digits are 74 but that means 7 is repeated. They cannot be 37.

If the last two digits are 47, the first two digits are 94 but that means 4 is repeated. They cannot be 47.

So the number can only be 5410827 and the middle digit is 0.

**YEAR 5 MATHEMATICAL REASONING**

## PRACTICE QUESTIONS

**1 B  2 B  3 A  4 D  5 C  6 C  7 C**   Page 30

1  Two beads are red. Three out of five is the same as six out of ten, so six of the beads will be blue. That leaves two beads, so two are white.

2  We are told that $\triangle \times 8 = 72$ so $\triangle = 9$ because 9 × 8 = 72. We are also told that $\square + \square + \triangle + \triangle + \triangle = 37$ so $2 \times \square + 3 \times 9 = 37$. As 3 × 9 = 27, $2 \times \square = 10$ and $\square = 5$.

3  The smallest three-digit whole number is 100. The largest four-digit whole number is 9999. Now, 100 + 9999 = 10 099.

4  The value of the digit 9 is 90 000 and that of the digit 3 is 300. 90 000 ÷ 300 = 300. It is 300 times larger.

5  100 is a multiple of both 2 and 5. 100 ÷ 5 = 20 so 100 is the 20th multiple of 5. There are 19 multiples of 5 between 1 and 99. 100 ÷ 2 = 50

so 100 is the 50th multiple of 2. There are 49 multiples of 2 between 1 and 99. Any multiples of both 2 and 5 are multiples of 10. There are 9 multiples of 10 between 1 and 99 so there are 9 multiples of both 2 and 5. Only statement Z is correct.

6   As there are five children who each collected a different number between 8 and 12, the numbers must be 8, 9, 10, 11 and 12. As Ruby got 8 and Danny 11, the others must have 9, 10 and 12 in some order. As Geri found more than Vinh but fewer than Nadia, Vinh had 9, Geri had 10 and Nadia 12. The only true statement is that Geri collected one more than Vinh.

7   The numbers in the first column add to 7 plus the bottom number. The numbers in the bottom row must also add to 7 plus that number. As 1 + 6 = 7, X must be 6.

| 4 | 9 | 2 |
| 3 | 5 | 7 |
| 8 | 1 | 6 |

**1 D  2 B  3 A  4 C  5 E**                    Page 32

1   Knowing that $5 \times 12 = 60$ and that 12 hours is half a day, we know that 60 hours is two and a half days. So 60 hours after 6:30 pm Friday will be 6:30 am Monday and 3 hours after that is 9:30 am Monday.

2   The length of each side of square B is 4 times that of square A so 4 square As will fit across square B and 4 will fit down. As $4 \times 4 = 16$, the area of square B is 16 times that of square A.

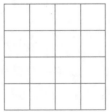

3   The scales show an amount weighing 350 g. But the plate weighs 210 g. As $350 - 210 = 140$, the amount of butter on the plate must be 140 g. Nathan needs 125 g. Now, $140 - 125 = 15$ so Nathan has 15 g more than he needs. He needs 15 g less.

4   The total length across the bottom must be the same as the total length across the top (20 m). Adding the bottom lengths that we know $(3.5 + 2.5 + 4.5)$ m = 10.5 m. So another 9.5 m is needed. X must be 9.5 m.

5   The area of P is $10 \times 4 = 40$ cm$^2$. Now, $8 \times 5 = 40$ so if the area of Q is the same as the area of P, the width of Q must be 5 cm. The perimeter of P is $2 \times (10 + 4)$ cm or 28 cm and the perimeter of Q is $2 \times (8 + 5)$ cm or 26 cm. So the perimeter of rectangle P is 2 cm more than the perimeter of rectangle Q.

**1 B  2 D  3 A**                    Page 34

1   Check each statement. Billy won, Ivan was second and Nabil was fourth. Henri jumped 3.8 m but Sam jumped 4.1 m, not 4.2 m.

2   The value for both chips and lollies is 10 so together they would make 20, making them the third most popular.

3   Consider each statement. Lauren's mark in week 4 was less than that of week 3 so statement 1 is not correct. The biggest improvement was where the graph is steepest, between weeks 4 and 5. So statement 2 is correct. Between weeks 5 and 9, Lauren scored at least 40 marks. If each test is marked out of 50, then statement 3 would be correct. We are not, however, given any information about what the test is marked out of so we cannot say that statement 3 must be correct.

## YEAR 5 READING **SAMPLE TEST**  Page 35

1 A  2 C  3 B  4 D  5 C  6 D  7 B  8 C  9 B
10 F  11 D  12 A  13 C  14 B  15 D  16 C
17 B  18 A  19 D  20 C

1   Mr Darling has 'a passion to be like his neighbours'.

   **The other options are incorrect.** These imply he does not want to be like his neighbours.

2   Nana policed other nursemaids' behaviour by checking on the children they were looking after in the park. If she found they'd been 'careless' in their care of them in any way, she would report this to their employers. No wonder they hated her!

   **A is incorrect.** Nana was clearly held in high regard in her own family.

   **B and D are incorrect.** There is no evidence the nursemaids were jealous of Nana or that she had threatened to bite them.

3   Nana's behaviour in her role as the children's nurse is consistently prim and proper. She makes the children behave well and ensures they are always dressed appropriately. Her 'sedate' walk and her role as their moral guardian earn this description.

   **A is incorrect.** She is not always gentle with the children or others involved with them.

   **C is incorrect.** She is resentful occasionally and can be crabby at times.

   **D is incorrect.** Although she is certainly thoughtful, this 'genius' can't be described as foolish.

4   It is very peculiar to trust the full-time care of your children to a dog. This makes the Darling family highly unusual. Their behaviour is quite the opposite of conventional, normal or typical. Therefore **A, B and C are incorrect**.

5   You can judge that in the real world a dog is unable to behave as Nana behaves in this story. It is pure fantasy.

**A is incorrect.** The relationship between Mr and Mrs Darling is like that of most married couples. Despite hiring a dog as a nursemaid, which is pure fantasy, their relationship itself is quite normal.

**B is incorrect.** This is a particular example of Nana's behaviour. It is her behaviour in general that marks the story as pure fantasy.

**D is incorrect.** We don't know what Mr Darling's associates would think and if we did, it is too little to confirm this is pure fantasy.

6   The poet states that Will is 'the strongest creature for his size' and also that 'He's neither shrewd nor clever'.

   **A is incorrect.** Will is intent on his tasks and takes no notice of others.

   **B is incorrect.** Although Will may be contented with his life, he is not at all lazy.

   **C is incorrect.** Although Will is annoying, there is no sense that his behaviour is designed to deliberately annoy.

7   As the poet says, 'Wombats dig forever' and Weary Will is no exception. He digs underground to make a home and when he wants to get to his haunts, he digs a hole under the fence. Nothing deters him.

   **A and C are incorrect.** There is no evidence the wombat is bored or depressed.

   **D is incorrect.** It is not suggested that the wombat wants to punish the stockman for his behaviour.

8   You can work out that a boundary rider's job is to check that fences stay in good order to keep dingoes and other predators from harming sheep or cattle on the property. When Will digs holes under the fence, dingoes are then able to get onto the property which is annoying to the boundary rider.

   **A is incorrect.** It would not annoy the boundary rider that Will kept going through the swinging gate. He had made it for that purpose so Will didn't need to dig a hole under the fence.

   **B is incorrect.** The boundary rider is not concerned with how Will is feeling but with what he is doing.

**D is incorrect**. While it is true that Will is not very clever, this is not what is annoying the boundary rider; rather it is Will's persistence in digging under the fence despite the obstacles put in his way.

9   You can judge that the poet tells the story of his 'battle' with Will with a wry humour. It is like a tall tale: there is truth in the story but it is exaggerated for effect. He is amused that Will has 'won' this battle without even realising he was a part of it. The comical rhymes in the poem (combat/wombat; burrow/thorough) are a part of this lighthearted attitude.

   **C is incorrect**. Although Will's actions irritate the boundary rider, he tells the story about them with humour and not irritation.

   **A and D are incorrect**. There is no sign of seriousness or pessimism in the way the story is told.

10  In the previous sentence the author is talking about what is characteristic of this species, such as the dolphin's small dorsal fins. This sentence is an aside about dorsal fins more generally: (Dorsal fins in dolphins are like thumb prints in humans—they can be used to identify individuals.) The sentence that follows goes back to what characterises the species: their melon-shaped heads without any beak.

11  In the previous sentence the author is talking about the coastal waters in Australia inhabited by snubfin dolphins. This sentence refers to where they can be found outside Australia: They are also found as far north as Papua New Guinea. The sentence that follows details the areas they favour within these waters: river and creek mouths.

12  In the previous sentence the author is talking about how dolphins sleep in a different way from humans. This sentence explains this difference: They allow one half of their brains to sleep at a time. The sentence that follows explains how this allows them to remain conscious at all times—something humans cannot do.

13  In the previous sentence the author is talking about a major threat to dolphins. This sentence refers to another major threat: Another major threat is habitat destruction. The sentence that follows gives more details about the kind of habitat destruction that causes risk to the dolphins' survival.

14  In the previous sentence the author is talking about the slow reproduction rate of dolphins, which is part of what makes them vulnerable to environmental threats. This sentence explains their breeding patterns: They don't begin to breed until aged about nine and produce only one calf every few years. The sentence that follows warns they could easily become an endangered species.

   The unused sentence is E.

15  In the review of the book *Circle*, the author notes there is a circle of life. How the environment is cared for affects the lives of all living things, including birds.

   **The other options are incorrect**. None of these texts explain why caring for the environment is important.

16  This is a radio broadcast. The language used is semi-formal as suits a news bulletin. Some sentences begin with 'And', which is more characteristic of spoken than written language, and it ends with a direct address: 'Well done, Leeland Primary.' A (a poem), B (a letter) and D (a review) are all written texts.

17  The eagle in the poem is poised high up on the mountain walls looking down at the sea below, waiting for a sight of its prey. The sea is so far beneath him that it looks as though its waves are mere wrinkles. The eagle perches proud and confident, then plunges down like a thunderbolt to capture his prey. This bird can see over a long distance with pinpoint accuracy.

   **The other options are incorrect**. They do not discuss the nature of the sight of the birds they describe.

18  Suki's letter includes the word 'ornithologist', which means someone who studies birds. Suki's uncle is an ornithologist, which is why

she writes to him about her own research about magpies.

**The other options are incorrect.** They do not include this term.

19 You can judge it is an extraordinary feat for a bird to fly from Alaska to Australia; then after feeding to fly back again. In other words, to circle the world.

**A is incorrect.** The eagle is able to spot his prey from a great distance but you can judge it is less extraordinary than the Bar-tailed Godwit's feat of circling the world.

**B is incorrect.** You can judge that for a magpie to be able to imitate a kookaburra is very clever but less extraordinary than the Bar-tailed Godwit's feat.

**C is incorrect.** For a duck to learn to walk with a prosthetic leg is a fine achievement but less extraordinary than the Bar-tailed Godwit's feat.

20 The use of a 3D printer enables the duck in the news item to have a new foot 'printed' and attached to its leg. This enables the duck to walk again.

**A and D are incorrect.** They do not refer to technology.

**B is incorrect.** Although email is a technology used in Suki's research into magpie behaviour, her research doesn't result in providing help to a magpie.

### YEAR 5 THINKING SKILLS SAMPLE TEST    Page 41

1 C  2 C  3 B  4 D  5 C  6 A  7 C  8 B  9 C
10 C  11 B  12 A  13 B  14 D  15 D  16 D
17 C  18 C  19 A  20 A

1 Jenny was first. Cheryn was second and Katie third. Tabatha was behind Katie but ahead of Myra so Tabatha came fourth.

2 If anyone who poisoned the tree must have had the opportunity and also the tree must have been blocking their view, then it follows that anyone who did not satisfy both requirements cannot have poisoned the tree.

So if the tree was not blocking Mr Smith's view, he cannot have poisoned it.

3 There are two different steps in this sequence. The first step is to multiply the number by 3 and the second step is to subtract 3.
So, $3 \times 4 = 12$ and $12 - 3 = 9$.
$3 \times 9 = 27$ and $27 - 3 = 24$
$3 \times 24 = 72$
As $72 - 3 = 69$, the next number is 69.

4 Neither Lola nor Conner's reasoning is correct. Lola says that Mimi will be a successful mountain climber 'for sure' and Mimi appears to have the qualities needed. However, the information does not say that someone with those qualities will **definitely** be a successful mountain climber. Lola's reasoning is therefore flawed.

Conner's reasoning is also flawed. He tells us that Finn is persistent and did not give up on cross-country even though he was not good at running. So **if** Finn **is** afraid of heights (Conner only says he **thinks** he is) and **if** fear of heights is an obstacle to mountain climbing, then Finn might be able to overcome that obstacle. So Conner cannot say mountain climbing is **definitely** not for Finn.

5 Imagine the figure flipped across the mirror line.

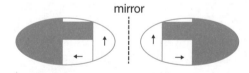

6 All the times show 59 minutes so only the hours need to be considered. 7 pm is 1900, 11 pm is 2300, 9 pm is 2100 and 9 am is 0900. $1 + 9$ gives a greater total than $2 + 3$, $2 + 1$ or $0 + 9$.

7 Ria's conclusion is that Na loves the cold because she goes swimming every morning at dawn when it is cold. For this conclusion to hold, it must be assumed that everyone who swims when it's cold loves the cold: Na goes swimming when it's cold + everyone who swims when it's cold loves the cold means therefore Na loves the cold.

**8** Olly's argument is that snakes should not be kept as pets because it's cruel to keep them in glass tanks instead of in their natural habitat. The fact that snakes don't generally like being held could strengthen his argument. However, the fact that snakes in captivity cannot engage in natural behaviours like burrowing, climbing trees or travelling long distances **most** strengthens his argument since it is about taking the snakes away from their natural habitat.

**9** All the cubes in the front layer can be seen and all those on the top and on the right side. There are 5 in the middle row and 5 on the bottom row that cannot be seen.

**10** From the information you can draw the conclusion that if Yusaf was hungry, he wouldn't play well. And if he didn't play well, there is no way he would be offered a place on the team.

**11** There will be 8 shows in the week beginning Friday 13 and another 8 in the week beginning Friday 20. There will be another show on Friday 27, 2 on Saturday 28 and 1 on Sunday 29. As $8 + 8 + 4 = 20$, there will be 20 shows altogether.

**12** Garage 5 cannot belong to Dane or Kahlia. Nor can it belong to Georgie or Alice. So Martin must have garage 5. Garage 4 cannot belong to Kahlia nor can it belong to Georgie or Alice. Dane must have garage 4. Garage 1 cannot belong to Kahlia or Alice. So Georgie must have garage 1. Kahlia's garage is between Georgie's and Alice's so Kahlia must have garage 2 and Alice garage 3.

**13** Arlo's mother's conclusion is that the sculpture park must be kept open. Her reason is that if the sculpture park closes, it will hurt the economy. For her conclusion to hold, it must be assumed we should not do something that will hurt the economy: If the sculpture park closes, it will hurt the economy + we should not do something that will hurt the economy means therefore the sculpture park must be kept open.

**14** The argument is that the voting age should be lowered to 16 because young people today are more mature and deserve to have a say on decisions that affect them. The statement that research shows the brains of 16 year olds are not fully mature weakens this argument.

**15** Kelly arrived at 9:30 am and Blake arrived at the same time. Finn arrived an hour before Blake so at 8:30 am. Alice arrived $\frac{1}{2}$ hour before Finn so at 8:00 am. Alice arrived $\frac{1}{2}$ hour after Natalie so Natalie arrived at 7:30 am. Amina arrived $2\frac{1}{2}$ hours after Natalie so at 10:00 am. Alice did arrive at 8:00 am, Natalie did arrive first, Amina did arrive $1\frac{1}{2}$ hours after Finn but Kelly did not arrive $1\frac{1}{2}$ hours after Natalie—she arrived 2 hours after Natalie.

**16** As $72 - 49 = 23$, there were 23 more cats than owners. This means that 23 owners had two cats. Now, $49 - 23 = 26$. All of the owners had either one or two cats so 26 owners had exactly one cat.

**17** Ying assumes that since six artworks by students won contests during the year, there were six students who created those artworks. However, it may be that some students won more than one art contest. In this case fewer than half of the qualifiers could be contest winners. So C shows the flaw in her reasoning.

**18** Rosie finished second but was slower than Fish. So Fish must have been first to finish the course. A and D could be true. B is true.

| Dog | Order finished | Obstacles cleared |
| --- | --- | --- |
| Fish | 1 | 7 |
| Maisie | 3 or 4 | 9 or 10 |
| Truffles | 5 | 10 |
| Rosie | 2 | 8 |
| Nugget | 3 or 4 | Not known |

**19** Only one person makes true statements. Vincent says Cooper is the youngest and Cooper also says he is the youngest. They can't both be telling the truth so must both be lying. If Paige is telling the truth, Ruby must be lying so cannot be the oldest. Vincent is lying so cannot be the oldest. Paige would be the youngest, not the oldest, and Vincent would be older than Cooper. Therefore nobody could be the oldest. This means Paige must also be lying. Ruby must be the person who is telling the truth.

**20** The argument is that reading a book is healthier than watching television because reading exercises your brain. A tells us television has a negative effect on the brain, which strengthens the argument that reading is healthier. D also supports the argument but it is a restatement of the information provided. Therefore A is the statement that most strengthens the argument.

### YEAR 5 MATHEMATICAL REASONING SAMPLE TEST

Page 45

> **1** A **2** B **3** C **4** A **5** B **6** E **7** C **8** D **9** D
> **10** C **11** B **12** A **13** E **14** B **15** D **16** E
> **17** B **18** E **19** D **20** D

**1** From the top there is 1 cube, then 2 cubes and then 3 cubes. So another 4 + 5 + 6 (or 15) cubes are needed.

**2** 9 marbles in each of 15 bags plus another 5 is 140. 9 × 15 + 5 = 140

**3** The perimeter of the shaded shape will be (4 + 4) cm greater than the original rectangle. 44 + 8 = 52.

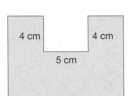
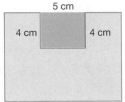

**4** Mary could roll a 4, 5 or 6 to get a larger number than Mick. So she has three chances out of six or one chance in two.

**5** The first car is (9 – 3) cm or 6 cm long. So the two cars will be 2 × 6 cm or 12 cm long.

**6** A pentagon has 5 sides. The prism will have 7 faces, 15 edges and 10 vertices. 7 + 15 + 10 = 32

**7**
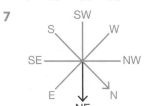

**8** When holding the dog, the scales show 74 kg. Without the dog, Nadine weighs 58 kg. The difference is the weight of the dog: 74 – 58 = 16.

**9** Remember: Multiplication and division should be done before adding and subtracting. If $\square$ = + and $\triangle$ = – then the sentence becomes 3 + 3 ÷ 3 + 3 – 3 which means 3 + 1 + 3 – 3 = 4. X is correct. If $\square$ = + and $\triangle$ = ÷ then the sentence becomes 3 + 3 ÷ 3 + 3 ÷ 3 which means 3 + 1 + 1 = 5. Y is not correct. If $\square$ = × and $\triangle$ = ÷ then the sentence becomes 3 × 3 ÷ 3 + 3 ÷ 3 which means 9 ÷ 3 + 1 or 3 + 1 which is 4. Z is correct.

**10** 3 of the blocks are grey. Now, $\frac{2}{5}$ is the same as $\frac{4}{10}$. So 4 of the 10 blocks will be white. This leaves 3 blocks so 3 will be black.

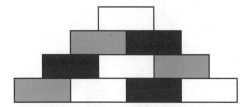

**11** Work backwards. Elaine's answer was 8. This was after subtracting 1, so before 1 was subtracted the answer was 9. This was after dividing by 2 so the answer was 18 before that. Before adding 3, it would have been 15 and before multiplying by 5 the number must have been 3.

**12** The difference in price for the cabins is $749 – $480 = $269. Joe would pay for 2 extra days skiing. Now, 2 × $15 = $30. So Joe's holiday would cost $299 more.

**13** 1425 is 25 minutes past 2 pm in 12-hour time. Three-quarters of an hour is 45 minutes. 35 minutes after 2:25 pm is 3 pm and 10 minutes after that is 3:10 pm.

**14** There are 14 boys and 16 girls so statement 1 is correct. The graph doesn't give any information about the height of the students so statement 2 is not correct. There are more girls than boys for each of the younger ages and more boys than girls for the older ages. So, on average, the boys tend to be older than the girls. Statement 3 is not correct.

**15** A triangular pyramid has four triangular faces. 2 and 3 can fold to form a triangular pyramid but 1 would fold to form a square-based pyramid.

**16** There are two different steps in this sequence. The first step is to double the number and the second step is to subtract 1.

So, 2 × 2 = 4 and 4 – 1 = 3.

2 × 3 = 6 and 6 – 1 = 5

2 × 5 = 10 and 10 – 1 = 9

2 × 9 = 18 and 18 – 1 = 17.

The next step is 2 × 17 = 34.

**17** There is only one line along which the figure could be folded and the two sides match exactly.

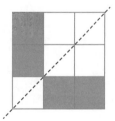

**18** Angus, Robbie and Carrie each collected more than 19 and fewer than 25 stamps. Angus collected two more than Robbie but one fewer than Carrie. So either Robbie found 20, Angus 22 and Carrie 23 or Robbie found 21, Angus 23 and Carrie 24. So B is not correct. A, C and D might be correct. The option that must be correct is E.

**19** The top of each can has radius 5 cm so diameter 10 cm. Six rows of 4 cans means that the rectangle has length 60 cm and width 40 cm. As 60 × 40 = 2400, the area is 2400 cm².

**20** One diagonal and the first column both have X. The other two numbers must add to the same total. As 28 is 1 less than 29, the middle number must be 1 more than 30. Now, comparing the other diagonal and the first column, they both have 30. 29 is 2 less than 31 so X must be 2 more than 32. (Or use the sum from the other diagonal: 30 + 31 + 32 = 93.)

| 30 | 35 | 28 |
| --- | --- | --- |
| 29 | 31 | 33 |
| 34 | 27 | 32 |

## PRACTICE QUESTIONS

1 A  2 C                                                    Page 51

1   Marilla is annoyed that Anne is asking to visit her friend Diana not long after she's been talking with her, at length, earlier in the day. Her annoyance shows in the way she describes them talking: 'tongues going the whole blessed time, clickety-clack'. In this context 'blessed' is like a swear word.

**B is incorrect.** Marilla doesn't see their time together as 'precious'.

**C is incorrect.** Marilla is referring to the particular half hour when their tongues were 'going'.

**D is incorrect.** The phrase 'the whole blessed time' refers to the length of time they didn't stop talking, not the way they talked.

2   Marilla sounds as if she'll refuse Anne's request as she thinks it unreasonable. However, she gives in once Anne uses the word 'suffering'. She still sets a limit on the time Anne is to spend at Diana's, making her response very fair in the circumstances.

**A and B are incorrect.** She lets Anne do what she is desperate to do.

**D is incorrect.** Although Marilla reveals something of a soft heart in relenting towards Anne, her response is given reluctantly and with sarcasm so cannot accurately be described as 'loving'.

1 A  2 B                                                    Page 54

1   When the poet views the bent, swaying boughs of the birch trees he likes to imagine they are that shape because boys have been swinging on them. He knows this is a romantic thought, however. He knows it is really nature, in the shape of ice-storms, that makes the birches bend 'down to stay': 'Ice storms do that'.

**B is incorrect.** While the poet's description of the trees covered in ice creates a magical scene, this is not what his words imply.

**C is incorrect.** The poet makes clear the boughs are not flexible enough to resist the ice-storms weighing them down.

**D is incorrect.** Although it is true the trees could not be ridden during ice-storms, this is not what the words imply.

2   The poet's words, spoken in a relaxed, natural way—'I like to think some boy's been swinging on them'—carry his great pleasure in thinking of this.

**The other options are incorrect.** These words suggest he has a negative attitude towards the image.

1 A  2 D  3 C                                               Page 57

1   In the previous sentence the author points out there is plenty of quicksand in Australia. The missing sentence describes the places where you are likely to find it: You usually find it where water and loose soil meet. The sentence that follows explains where conditions of this kind are usually found.

2   In the previous sentence the author outlines the composition of quicksand and what happens when the water in this composition can't escape. The missing sentence tells what happens when weight is placed on the quicksand: This type of soil is unable to support weight. The sentence that follows explains what happens when a human being puts weight on quicksand.

3   In the previous sentence the author states that human beings do not drown in quicksand. The missing sentence gives the reason for this: Humans are not as dense as quicksand. The sentence that follows suggests how far they are likely to sink.

The unused sentence is B.

**1** B  **2** B  **3** A  Page 60

1   The reference to Bligh performing 'one of the most remarkable boat-voyages on record' is evidence of an extraordinary achievement. Text A does not refer to any extraordinary achievements.

2   Bligh's and Christian's views of what Christian is about to do are directly opposed to each other. Text A only gives Bligh's view of events.

3   Bligh lists the names or positions of all those who stand against him: Fletcher Christian, the master at arms, the gunner's mate, seaman Thomas Burkitt and the sentinels guarding those who were not of Christian's party. This shows he was outnumbered. Text B does not refer to the individuals involved in securing Bligh's defeat.

### YEAR 6 THINKING SKILLS

## PRACTICE QUESTIONS

**1** B  **2** A  **3** D  **4** C  Page 69

1   If the person who put the inflatable Santa Claus on the roof overnight must have had both an opportunity and a motive, then anyone who does not have both an opportunity and a motive can't have been the person who did it.

**A is incorrect**. Just because a person has an opportunity and a motive, it does not mean they must have done it.

**C is incorrect**. Scarlet might have had an opportunity but not a motive.

**D is incorrect**. Scarlet might have had a motive but still not have done it.

2   Jarrod concludes that the fire brigade is taking a long time to arrive. To draw this conclusion he must have assumed that someone has called the fire brigade (because he hasn't) and because a house is burning and other people in the crowd were already watching the fire when he joined them. He takes it for granted (without any proof or evidence) that the fire brigade has been called.

**B is incorrect**. Jarrod might have wondered if the fire truck was held up in traffic but this is not the assumption he made when he drew his conclusion that the fire truck was taking a long time to arrive.

**C and D are incorrect**. There's no evidence for Jarrod to have made these assumptions.

3   Jeremy says Lauren loves gymnastics and it helps keep her fit for dancing. His argument would be strengthened by any further reasons for Lauren to continue with gymnastics. If both dancing and gymnastics require the skills of balance and coordination, then continuing to do gymnastics would be beneficial to Lauren's dancing career.

**A is incorrect.** The statement that these skills are used in gymnastics does not strengthen the argument that continuing with gymnastics will support Lauren's dancing.

**B is incorrect**. This is a side issue and does not strengthen the argument that Lauren should continue with gymnastics.

**C is incorrect**. This might be true but it argues that dancing keeps you fit for gymnastics instead of addressing Lauren's concern that she needs to focus on dancing instead of dividing her time between gymnastics and dancing.

4   Travis's reasoning is correct when he points out that the animal's skin is not smooth like a frog's and its legs are short like a toad's but he still only says he thinks it **could** be a toad. He does not say it **is** a toad. This shows a level of uncertainty and means he's allowing that it could possibly be a frog.

**A is incorrect**. Viggo has concluded that the animal is a frog because it's walking. The information tells you that frogs prefer to hop or jump so Viggo is incorrect. He also uses incorrect reasoning to assert that he knows something is true when he is basing his conclusion on inconclusive, vague evidence.

**B is incorrect**. Gillian is incorrect to state that the animal is a toad based on its smooth skin when the information tells you that toads have dry warty-looking skin and frogs have smooth skin.

**D is incorrect.** Haruna uses incorrect reasoning to assert that she's sure it's a frog based on the vague evidence that the animal is walking and 'not that warty looking'.

**1 D  2 B  3 C  4 C**    Page 71

1  A mirror image is a reflection. Imagine the whole sign reflected or flipped over a vertical line.

2  We can see that there are four tiles across and four down. Looking carefully we can see that the four tiles in each column and the four in each row all have different orientations. The missing tile is the one in option B.

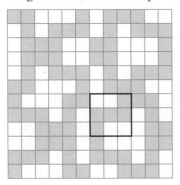

3  The blocks in options A, B and D are used.

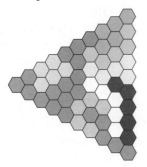

4  The oval shape (O) is not used. One rectangle (R), one square (S) and four quadrants (Q) (quarters of a circle) are used.

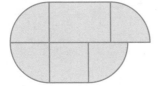

**1 A  2 D  3 A  4 A**    Page 73

1  To answer this question, look for contradictions in the given statements. Harry and Ethan gave contradictory statements. They cannot both be true and they cannot both be false. One statement must be true and the other must be false. So the runner who makes the true statement is either Harry or Ethan. This means both Travis and Mitch must be wrong. Travis said he did not win and, because that is wrong, Travis must have won. (If Travis won, then Ethan's statement must have been the correct one because Harry's statement that Ethan won must have been false.)

2  All the statements are false. So Brittany doesn't have the green, purple or blue marble. Brittany's marble is red. Daniel doesn't have the purple or green marbles and cannot have red. So Daniel's marble is blue. Chloe doesn't have the purple or red marble and cannot have the blue. So her marble is green.

3  If Isabella is telling the truth, Keith isn't lying so he is also telling the truth. Only one is telling the truth so that person is not Isabella. So the statement 'Keith isn't lying' is false and Keith is lying. Therefore Keith's statement 'Ruth is lying' is false and Ruth is the person telling the truth.

4  To answer this question, sort through the given statements and look for contradictions. At least one of the two statements is true so both statements could be true but both statements cannot be false. If he did not score 36 runs, then the true statement made to Ken must be that he took no wickets and the true statement made to Luke must be that he took two wickets. That is a contradiction: he cannot have taken both no wickets and two wickets. The correct statement made to both Ken and Luke is that he scored 36 runs and the correct statement made to Joe is that he did not score 56 runs. The statement that must be true is he scored 36 runs.

**1** B  **2** C  **3** D  **4** D  **5** D     Page 75

**1** Some students study chemistry alone. All students studying biology must also study chemistry. So more students study chemistry than biology. Similarly all students studying physics are also studying chemistry so more students study chemistry than study physics. So either chemistry or geology is the subject that has the most students. Any student who studies geology and physics must also be studying chemistry. Any students studying both geology and chemistry will be counted in both subjects so will not affect the difference in numbers. More students study chemistry alone than geology alone so more students in total must study chemistry than study geology. Chemistry is the subject that has the most students.

**2** Total probability of red, blue, yellow and green must be 1. Now, if the probability of red or yellow is the same as the probability of blue and green then both those probabilities must be 0.5. As the number of red marbles is four times the number of yellow, the probability of red is also four times the probability of yellow. So the probability of red is 0.4 and the probability of yellow is 0.1. The probability of blue is twice that of yellow so it is 0.2, meaning the probability of green is 0.5 − 0.2 or 0.3.

**3** As Mitchell's age is three times Nathan's, the difference in their ages is two times Nathan's age. That difference, however, is 12 years. So Nathan is 6 and Mitchell is 18. The sum of all the ages is 6 × 6 or 36. As 6 + 18 = 24 and 36 − 24 = 12, Jack must be 12.

**4** The unknown scores in round 5 are 2, 3, 4 and 5. Atticus finished in first place with 6 + 4 + 1 + 3 + 6 = 20 points. Maeve finished in sixth place with 5 + 2 + 3 + 4 + 1 = 15 points. Now, as no two children had the same number of total points, the remaining four must have, in some order, 16, 17, 18 and 19 points. Oscar finished third so must have 18 total points.

Now, 3 + 3 + 6 + 1 = 13 so he has 13 points from rounds 1 to 4. As 18 − 13 = 5, he must have got 5 points from round 5.

The completed table would be as follows:

| Name | Round 1 | Round 2 | Round 3 | Round 4 | Round 5 | Position |
|---|---|---|---|---|---|---|
| Atticus | 6 | 4 | 1 | 3 | 6 | 1 |
| Chloe | 4 | 1 | 5 | 2 | 4 | 5 |
| Elias | 1 | 5 | 2 | 6 | 3 | 4 |
| Kane | 2 | 6 | 4 | 5 | 2 | 2 |
| Maeve | 5 | 2 | 3 | 4 | 1 | 6 |
| Oscar | 3 | 3 | 6 | 1 | 5 | 3 |

**5** First change each of Georgia's words into code, remembering that each letter will be replaced by a number from between 1 and 26.

L is 12, I is 9, O is 15 and N is 14 so LION will be 1291514.

M is 13, U is 21, S is 19 and T is 20 so MUST will be 13211920.

P is 16, L is 12, O is 15 and D is 4 so PLOD will be 1612154.

S is 19, A is 1, V is 22 and E is 5 so SAVE will be 191225.

Then each of those numbers needs to be examined to see if it could be another word.

Remember: The question stated that the words were simple so you can quickly eliminate many of the possibilities.

Instead of SAVE (19 1 22 5), Georgia could have found SLY (19 12 25).

No different, simple words can be found instead of LION, MUST or PLOD.

The word for which Georgia found a different word was SAVE.

### YEAR 6 MATHEMATICAL REASONING

## PRACTICE QUESTIONS

**1** D **2** B **3** A **4** E **5** C **6** B　　Page 77

**1**　There are 800 seats altogether and 270 in Theatre 1. The number of seats in Theatres 2 and 3 combined is 800 − 270 or 530. If there were 150 more seats, there would be the same number in Theatre 2 and Theatre 3. Now, 530 + 150 = 680. Half of that number is 680 ÷ 2 = 340. There are 340 seats in Theatre 2.

**2**　5 oranges = 5 × 4 quarters = 20 quarters. Total quarters eaten = 2 + 5 + 3 + 6 = 16. So Daniel ate 4 quarters, 2 more than Susan. As $\frac{2}{4} = \frac{1}{2}$, Daniel ate half an orange more than Susan.

**3**　The lounge is half of the price of the table and chairs. So the lounge is one-third of the total price. As $1650 ÷ 3 = $550, the lounge costs $550 so the dining table and chairs cost $1100. As the dining table is $100 less than the chairs, subtracting $100 will be double the price of the dining table.
Now, $1100 − $100 = $1000 and half of $1000 is $500, so the dining table costs $500.

**4**　6 and 7 have no factors in common (apart from 1) so their common multiples less than 100 are 6 × 7 or 42 and 2 × 6 × 7 or 84. Now, all multiples of 6 are even and the digits add up to 6 or a multiple of 6. So 96 is the largest number less than 100 that is a multiple of 6. As 96 ÷ 6 = 16, there are 16 multiples of 6 between 1 and 100. Two of those are also multiples of 7 so there are 14 that are multiples of 6 but not multiples of 7.

**5**　Caleb and Ty got the same mark so they must have scored 87. Ty got a lower mark than Emma so Emma must have got 89 or 92. Hailey's mark was lower than David's but higher than Lewis's. So David must have scored 92 or 89, Hailey must have scored 83 and Lewis must have scored 80. So the statements in options A, B, D and E must all be true. The statement 'Emma scored 92' might be true but it also might not be true.

**6**　From Riley, Brad can buy two pies for $10 and get the third one free. So he would pay $10 for 3 and $20 for 6. From Samantha, Brad would pay 6 × $3 or $18 for 6 pies. From Harrison, Brad would get two pies for $8 and the third one for $2. So he would pay $20 for 6 pies. From Stephen, Brad would get 5 pies for 5 × $3.80 and the sixth one free. So he would pay $19 for 6 pies. Brad can buy 6 pies for the least amount from Samantha.

**1** C **2** C **3** D **4** A **5** A **6** D　　Page 79

**1**　The mass of a large tub is five times that of a small tub and the difference in mass is 560 g. But the difference is four times the mass of a small tub. Now, 560 ÷ 4 = 140. So the mass of the small tub is 140 g. As 5 × 140 = 700, the mass of the large tub is 700 g. A box holds five of the large tubs. 5 × 700 = 3500. So the box weighs 3500 g or 3.5 kg.

**2**　The difference in perimeter is an extra 1.5 m at the top and bottom of each side of the doubles court. So the width of the doubles court is 3 m larger and the total perimeter is 6 m larger.

**3**　The width of the singles court is 11 m − 3 m or 8 m. The length is 2 × (5.5 + 6.5) m or 24 m. So the area is 24 × 8 or 192 m$^2$.

**4**　The total distance travelled is 2 × (48 + 52 + 49 + 95 + 56) km or 600 km. Time taken = (600 ÷ 80) or 7.5 hours.

**5**　February is the only month with just 28 days. So 'last month' is April and 'this month' is May. The next month containing the letter 'r' is September but September only has 30 days. October is the first month with 31 days.

**6**　Volume = 2 × 2 × 2 = 8 cm$^3$. The mass is 1.5 g for each cm$^3$. 1.5 × 8 = 8 + 4 = 12. So the mass is 12 g.

1 B  2 C  3 C  4 C  Page 81

1 The chart is divided into 3 parts, 6 parts, 4 parts and 5 parts. Now, looking at the table, the numbers are all multiples of 4. So dividing by 4 we get 4 for apple, 7 for banana, 5 for grapes, 6 for orange and 3 for peach. The chart shows peach then orange then apple then grapes. Banana must be the fruit that has been left out.

2 Read the values and categories carefully and write down the changes: the cost of the Claytons machine drops to $690 when the $110 is taken off. The Ayrtons Whitegoods machine drops to $675 and is cheapest (10% off = $75 from $750).

3 In January and April the total amount of more rain that fell in 1900 compared to what fell in 1899 is roughly the same as the amount of more rain that fell in February 1899 compared to February 1900. So we only need to consider March (difference just over 50), May (difference 50) and June (difference 40). Roughly 140 mm more fell in the first six months in 1900 than 1899.

4 The start of the pie chart is correct so Pia must have one-quarter of the total number. As $4 \times 30 = 120$, the total number must be 120. Now, $30 + 10 + 25 + 40 = 105$ and $120 - 105 = 15$. So the missing number for Ava must be 15. This is half the number for Pia so the angle size for Ava must be half of that for Pia. Half of $90°$ is $45°$.

**YEAR 6 READING SAMPLE TEST**  Page 82

1 D  2 A  3 B  4 B  5 A  6 B  7 A  8 C  9 D
10 F  11 B  12 A  13 C  14 E  15 B  16 C
17 A  18 D  19 C  20 D

1 The context suggests things are looking up for the men. They hadn't lost any dogs overnight, as they had been doing recently, and their spirits had lifted. This implies things were looking more promising that morning.

**The other options are incorrect.** None of these definitions fit the context.

2 One Ear thinks the she-wolf is waiting for him and he moves towards her in a 'mincing' walk and looks at her 'desirefully'.

**B is incorrect.** The men are playful rather than angry with the dogs when their sledge is overturned.

**C and D are incorrect.** There is no evidence for either statement in the text.

3 At this stage of the story, the she-wolf senses the men would protect One Ear and her best hope of trapping him is to lure him away.

**A and D are incorrect.** Although the she-wolf does want to please One Ear and show off her attractions, her main purpose in doing so is to lure him away from the men.

**C is incorrect.** There is no evidence she wants to worry him in the text.

4 One Ear does learn the wolf pack is getting closer but this is something the she-wolf knew well before he did. They are her pack and they communicate with each other.

**A is incorrect.** Both One Ear and the she-wolf know the men will try to protect their dog against the wolves.

**C and D are incorrect.** There is no evidence that the men plan to betray One Ear—in fact the opposite is true of Bill, in particular—and there is no evidence they have any knowledge of who can run faster.

5 At the end of the text it looks as if the she-wolf will trap One Ear while the rest of the wolves are moving dangerously closer. Then Bill decides to intervene to save their dog, which could be dangerous and foolhardy. Not knowing how these incidents are resolved means the text ends on a high point of tension.

**B and C are incorrect.** Although the reader may feel pessimistic or despairing about One Ear's and Bill's chance of survival as the story unfolds, this is not the note the extract finishes on. It ends with the reader not knowing what is going to happen next.

**D is incorrect.** There is nothing triumphant about the ending of the text.

6   The glass case is where the bird will stay forever: it is literally in a tomb, a place where the dead are buried.

**A is incorrect**. It is not the glass which stops the bird from flying away.

**C and D are incorrect**. While each statement is true, neither explains why the poet sees the bird as 'entombed' rather than, for example, on show or display.

7   The bird's feet are 'snap-fine' in the sense they are so thin they could shatter. This means the bird could easily be broken or destroyed; its fragility is emphasised.

**B is incorrect**. Although the bird may be photogenic, the words 'snap-fine feet' don't convey this idea.

**C is incorrect**. The bird is forever still and its sprightliness cannot be judged.

**D is incorrect**. The words 'snap-fine feet' are not an indication of perfection.

8   The poet finds it distressing to see so beautiful a living creature turned into a specimen for people to gaze at. She emphasises that seeing the bird unable to move or sing is painful for the viewer and robs the bird of its identity.

**A is incorrect**. While her feelings may include irritation, they carry more condemnation for what has happened than this word suggests.

**B and D are incorrect**. She does not describe experiencing any pleasure (appreciation or delight) from her visit.

9   The last word of the poem, 'this', has a heavy stress to emphasise the poet's distaste for the sight in front of her. She states that any other destiny for the bird would have been better. To end up preserved unnaturally in a glass case and trapped forever for people to look at is a travesty.

**A and C are incorrect**. It is not the death of the bird that the poet is emphasising.

**B is incorrect**. The poet thinks its burial ('better to know you nourish the soil / with your brittle bones') would be better than this entrapment in a glass case.

10   In the previous sentence the author is talking about how Nero used emeralds to improve his sight. This sentence explains that no-one really understands how this process worked for Nero: No-one is quite sure why this worked for him but it did. The sentence that follows gives another unusual example used by the Greeks to help them see small print.

11   In the previous sentence the author is talking about the next step in developing ways to improve eyesight: two glasses riveted together. This sentence explains how they could be made to stay on the face: They could be held or worn on the face by pinching them tightly onto the nose. The sentence that follows states what kind of material was used to house the glass.

12   In the previous sentence the author is talking about the shift towards using temple frames to keep glasses in place on the face. This sentence points out the advantages of this: This meant you could wear glasses and leave your hands free. The sentence that follows tells you who you could buy these glasses from at that time.

13   In the previous sentence the author is talking about the introduction of eye examinations to prescribe glasses. This sentence describes an early significant example: In 1862 a Dutch ophthalmologist developed an eye chart to measure clarity of vision. The sentence that follows points out that this eye chart is still used today.

14   In the previous sentence the author is talking about how wearing glasses has become quite fashionable. This sentence explains that some people even wear them when they don't need to improve their sight: Some people now wear glasses without prescription lenses because they think they make them look attractive. The sentence that follows explains another reason for the popularity of wearing glasses in modern times.

The unused sentence is D.

15 The text is written in the first person. We learn the writer is a horse and the text begins with his first memory. You can work out it is the beginning of his life's story—his autobiography.

**The other options are incorrect.** They are not told in the first person and not as part of a life story.

16 This is the only text with an exchange between an animal and a human. It is amusing to hear Dot and the Kangaroo talking about the subject of thinking, especially when the Kangaroo says she never does and that she prefers to 'jump' to conclusions. The pun on the word 'jump' is designed to make the reader smile.

**The other options are incorrect.** They do not include humorous elements.

17 Mole is captivated by his first sight of the river. He is 'bewitched, entranced, fascinated' by this sinuous 'animal' that chatters to him and tells him stories.

**The other options are incorrect.** While none of the animals in these texts express discontent, neither do they express delight.

18 There is no reference to water in this text.
**The other options are incorrect.** They all refer to water: Text A to 'a full-fed river'; Text C to water in the waterhole; and Text B to a pond of clear water.

19 The Kangaroo shows concern about Dot's distress and puts herself out by planning to carry Dot in her pouch to the river because she is thirsty.

**The other options are incorrect.** The animals in these texts do not have opportunities to show whether they can be kind or not.

20 Although one of the animal characters in this text is spoken of as a gentleman, his sandy whiskers and long bushy tail give away the fact that he is a fox in disguise.

**Text A is incorrect.** There is only one animal character included. The river is compared to a 'sleek, sinuous, full-bodied animal' but it is a river, not an animal.

**Text B is incorrect.** It is about a human and an animal, not two animals.

**Text D is incorrect.** It is has only one animal character.

## YEAR 6 THINKING SKILLS **SAMPLE TEST**

1 A  2 A  3 B  4 B  5 C  6 D  7 C  8 A  9 C
10 D  11 B  12 A  13 D  14 B  15 D  16 D
17 B  18 A  19 D  20 C

1 From the middle rung the cleaner climbs up 4 rungs, down 6 rungs, up 8 rungs and up 5 rungs to the top. So they climbed up a total of 17 rungs and down 6 rungs. This means the top rung is 11 rungs above the middle rung. There will also be 11 below the middle, plus the middle rung itself: 23 rungs in all.

2 Kahliah has concluded that the elderly man has dementia because the shopkeeper is talking to him like he's a child. She bases her conclusion on the evidence that the shopkeeper speaks to the man loudly and clearly. Kahliah must have assumed that you should talk to a person with dementia like you would talk to a child.

3 The missing part is two squares across and three down so each of the options would need to be rotated to fit. The top left square needs to be blue after the rotation. The triangular shapes are rotating in a clockwise direction from one corner of a square to the next as you move across each row. So the top right square of the missing piece needs a triangle in the bottom left corner. The bottom right square of the missing piece needs a triangle in the bottom right corner.

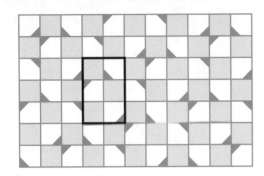

4   The main argument is that agritourism is a way for farmers to get their crops picked by tourists rather than have them rot in the fields. The statement that strengthens the argument is that agritourism is a win for the farmers (by preventing wastage) and a win for people wanting fresh produce.

5   Emma's reasoning is incorrect. The information states that at times the natural disaster occurs too suddenly to provide time for advance warning.

6   162 – 15 = 147 won medals. Four won 3 medals so 143 won either 1 or 2. There were 213 medals altogether so 213 – 4 × 3 = 201 were won by those who won either 1 or 2. Now, 201 – 143 = 58 so 58 more medals were won than people who won them. This means that 58 people won 2 medals.

7   Rhiannon has 6 more marbles than when she started. So for her turn she must have spun an even number and received 2 marbles from Isla and 2 from Petria. Rhiannon must have also received a marble from Isla and Petria from both of their spins.

Rhiannon would have been the only one to spin an even number. Isla and Petria would have both spun odd numbers and would have both given 3 marbles to Rhiannon. Isla would have also given a marble to Petria at her turn but received it back when Petria had her turn.

Both Isla and Petria would have lost 3 marbles altogether. They would both have 22 marbles.

8   The argument states that small mammals are threatened by predators and the only hope to save various species is the creation of predator-free areas. You can conclude that

while feral foxes and cats roam in the environment it's not safe there for small native mammals. B is incorrect because this statement is a fact in the text and not a conclusion drawn from the text. C and D are incorrect because these provide additional information not included in the text and are not conclusions possible to be drawn from the text.

9   The argument is that the Munga-Thirri–Simpson Desert National Park is a globally significant environmental area which should be protected for the future. The fact that when it rains, the Munga-Thirri temporary wetlands abound with bird life and native flowers strengthens that argument.

10  Theo finished before Keely and also before Victoria as Keely and Victoria finished at the same time. Mia finished after Keely so she also finished after Victoria and after Theo. Jackson finished after Mia and hence after Keely, Victoria and Theo. So Jackson finished last and took 55 min. Jackson finished 15 min after Victoria and Keely so they took 40 min. Theo finished 10 min before Keely so he finished in 30 min, 25 min before Jackson. So the sentences in A, B and C are all true. Now, Mia finished after Keely and before Jackson so she took between 40 min and 55 min but there is no further information to determine the exact time that Mia took. The sentence that might not be true is 'Mia finished in 50 min'.

11  Labradors can easily be found on the graph because that is the highest number. It is the second bar. The number of labradors is equal to the number of chihuahuas plus the number of terriers so these must be represented by the third and fourth bars in some order. But there are twice as many terriers as poodles so terriers cannot be the third bar. They must be the fourth bar and the poodles must be the first bar. Kelpies must be the last bar. So the statement in option B is not true. There are more terriers than kelpies, not more kelpies than terriers.

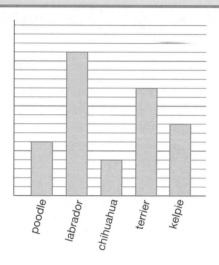

**12** There were no shows on Mondays so there were shows on 6 days a week. Saturdays and Sundays had 2 shows so there was a total of 8 shows each week. From Wednesday 1 September until Tuesday 28 September is 4 weeks. Now, 4 × 8 = 32. So there were 32 shows until 28 September and another show on Wednesday 29 September and another on Thursday 30 September. This means there were 34 shows altogether. If 1 September was a Wednesday so was 15 September and then 17 September was a Friday, 18 September was a Saturday and 19 September was a Sunday. This means Rhonda missed 5 shows. The number of shows Rhonda appeared in is 34 − 5 or 29.

**13** Ruth has used flawed or incorrect reasoning when she says that, despite being fully vaccinated two years ago, she still caught the flu this year. The information states that the flu viruses vary slightly from year to year so you need a new flu vaccination every year to maintain effective cover.

**14** Minnie Pwerle was a more popular name for the building than Ricky Maynard, which was more popular than Tracey Moffatt. Tracey Moffatt was preferred over Albert Namatjira and Sally Gabori. The result of the vote would have been to name the building The Minnie Pwerle Arts Building, after Minnie Pwerle.

**15** Anton's argument is that horseriding is dangerous and people don't understand the dangers. The statement that you can reduce your risk of injury from a fall by wearing protective clothing, learning about horses' behaviour and improving your ability as a rider weakens his argument.

**A is incorrect.** This may be true but does not weaken the argument that horseriding is dangerous.

**B is incorrect.** This information somewhat weakens the argument but not as much as D. If people with disabilities can ride horses safely, you could infer that it cannot be as dangerous as Anton states.

**C is incorrect.** This information strengthens Anton's argument.

**16** Xavier does not have native plants because he is furthest from the front. He doesn't deal with grasses because that is Mr Armstrong who is beside him. He doesn't handle the garden equipment because that is the work of Natasha. He does not sit next to Ms Watson so does not have vegetables. So Xavier must look after the flowers.

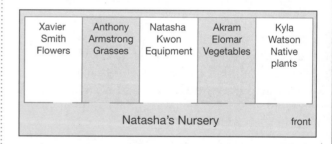

**17** If Wilson is properly trained, then whenever he is told to sit he must sit. At time 1, Wilson has been told to sit so the result P needs to be known. Also if Wilson doesn't sit, he must not have been told to sit. He didn't sit at time 3 so the result R needs to be known.

At time 2, Wilson was not told to sit so it doesn't matter whether he sits or not. At time 4, Wilson did sit so it doesn't matter whether he was told to or not. (Wilson is not only allowed to sit when told to.) So the results Q and S do not need to be known.

**18** Tyla has made an assumption about the road Jade will use to enter town. The evidence indicating Tyla has made this assumption is that she gives Jade driving directions to her new home based on this assumption. Tyla has assumed something to be true (the road Jade will use to enter town) without any proof or evidence. She hasn't confirmed with Jade her direction of travel but instead has taken it for granted that she knows which road Jade will use to enter town. Tyla might know where Jade lives in relation to the town but Jade may plan to enter town from a different direction or on a different road—so the instructions could be misleading.

**19** If the person who left the gate open must have had both an opportunity and a reason, then anyone who didn't have both of those can't have been the person to leave the gate open.

**20** If the present was in box 1, then both sentences on box 1 would be false. But at least one sentence must be true so the present cannot be in box 1. If the present was in box 3, then the second sentences on both boxes 2 and 3 would be false. The first sentence of both those boxes would therefore have to be true. But the present is for only one of Samara's children. Both first sentences cannot be true so the present cannot be in box 3. The present must be in box 2. The present is for either Ali or Mo so either A or B will be true but it is not correct to say they must be true.

**YEAR 6 MATHEMATICAL REASONING SAMPLE TEST**

Page 94

1 D 2 C 3 A 4 D 5 A 6 B 7 E 8 B 9 A
10 C 11 D 12 E 13 B 14 B 15 A 16 D
17 C 18 E 19 D 20 C

**1** Note that each layer has successive square numbers. The pattern of layers from the top is: $1 \times 1 = 1$, $2 \times 2 = 4$, $3 \times 3 = 9$, $4 \times 4 = 16$, and so on. One more layer at the bottom would need $7 \times 7 = 49$ blocks.

**2** If Sam is 19, he would be 20 ($4 \times 5$) next year and 21 ($3 \times 7$) the year after.

**3** The protractor shows that the top half of the angle is 50°. The design is symmetrical so the whole angle will be $2 \times 50°$ or 100°.

**4** There is one chance in 6 of rolling any number on a dice. So statement 1 is not correct. Half the numbers on the dice are even and half are odd. So statement 2 is correct. There are two numbers less than 3 so there are two chances in six, or one in three, of rolling a number less than 3. Statement 3 is correct.

**5** Adding the second row the total is 150. The missing number in the third column must be 39. The diagonal from the top left to the bottom right can then be completed, meaning the number at the bottom of the fourth column must be 45. So the number at the top of the fourth column, X, must be 33.

| 30 | 43 | 44 | 33 |
|----|----|----|----|
| 41 | 36 | 35 | 38 |
| 37 | 40 | 39 | 34 |
| 42 | 31 | 32 | 45 |

**6** Break the time down into seconds. Freddy takes 80 seconds per lap so 6 laps will take 480 seconds. In that time Cathy will have completed 9 laps ($9 \times 50 = 450$, $10 \times 50 = 500$).

**7** The diameter of the larger circle is 6 cm and the diameter of the smaller circle is 4 cm. The rectangle will be 10 cm long and 6 cm wide. So the area is $10 \times 6 = 60$ cm².

**8** The motorboat cost four times as much as the trailer so the total price is $4 + 1$ or five times the price of the trailer. Now, $6060 \div 5 = 1212$. So the trailer cost $1212 and the motorboat was $4848.

9   Being a regular pentagon, each side is $\frac{1}{5}$ or 20% of the distance around. Side A will be 20% or 0.2, B another 0.2 (making 0.4), Side C another 0.2 (making 0.6), so 0.65 will fall on Side D.

10  4 hours after 8:30 am is 12:30 pm and $\frac{3}{4}$ of an hour (or 45 minutes) after that is 1:15 pm. So the plane lands at 1:15 pm Sydney time which is 11:15 am Perth time. Another 45 minutes after that is 12 noon.

11  1691, 8008 and 8698 all look the same when rotated 180°. 6006 will not look the same.

12  Together Zoe, Doug and Suzy ate three apples. Mel ate one so there was one left. Yaz also ate one. So Mel and Yaz ate the same amount and Yaz ate twice as much as Suzy. One-half is two-quarters so Zoe ate $\frac{1}{4}$ more than Suzy. All the statements are correct.

13  Two-fifths of the spaces are for trucks. Now, $\frac{2}{5} = \frac{4}{10}$ and $\frac{4}{10}$ of 1000 = 400.

So 600 spaces are for cars. Three-quarters of 600 is 450.

14  January had about 20 mm and March about 80 mm so statement X is correct. They are the driest and wettest months and the difference is about 60 mm or 6 cm so statement Y is correct. May had just over 40 mm and June had just under 60 mm so together they had about 100 mm of rain. 1 m = 1000 mm. So statement Z is not correct.

15  The goods train travels at half the speed of the express train so will go half the distance in the same time. When the express train has gone 440 km, the goods train will have gone 220 km so will be between Q and H.

16  Six people bought three ice creams each. Now, 39 – 6 = 33 so 33 people bought either one or two ice creams. As 6 × 3 = 18 and 64 – 18 = 46, those 33 people bought a total of 46 ice creams. Now, 46 – 33 = 13. So there were 13 more ice creams bought than the number of people so 13 people must have bought an extra ice cream. Now, 33 – 13 = 20 so 20 people bought one ice cream.

17  There is 900 mL of drink in the jug. One part nectar and five parts lemonade means six parts altogether. Now, 900 ÷ 6 = 150 so Ned used 150 mL of nectar.

18  The last of the given numbers is 13. Using the rule, Q + 12 – 7 = 13 so Q + 5 = 13 and Q = 8. The next number will be 12 + 13 – 8 or 17.

19  The increase in perimeter is 192 cm – 144 cm or 48 cm. The perimeter has increased by four times the width of a paver.

Now, 48 ÷ 4 = 12 so the width of each paver is 12 cm.

20  Xavier got two more blue and two more green ribbons than Maxine and 14 more points. So together a blue and a green ribbon must be worth 7 points. If a green ribbon was worth 1 point, a blue would be worth 6 but 5 blue and 8 green would be worth 38 points not 44. Trying each of the options, the only one that will work is if a blue ribbon is worth 4 points and a green ribbon is worth 3 points.